WHY I'LL NEVER LIVE IN
OZ AGAIN

WHY I'LL NEVER LIVE IN
OZ AGAIN

...OR THE UK,
THE US, CANADA
OR NEW ZEALAND,
FOR THAT MATTER

Other books by Two Dogs:

Coming soon…

TWO DOGS
Books men read

Fix the tap. Clean the car. Argue with your boss. Grab a cold beer with friends on the way home from work. Watch the rugby. Put the children to bed. Argue with your bank on the internet. Call the plumber to fix the tap properly. Listen to "I told you so." Polish your shoes. Make up with your girl. Go to bed.

Two Dogs publishes books men read. So join us in getting stuck into the Big Fs – fitness, friendship, fast cars, fashion, food and fornication – plus a whole lot of stuff that leaves the F off.

Two Dogs publishes books you're as likely to be seen with on the beach or in the pub as you are with your feet up at home. Quick reads, long reads, books you can dip into, books you can get your teeth into, pages you can flick through again while you're waiting for her to finish her hair. "Does my bum look big in this?" Shhh! I'm reading. This is Two Dogs.

Some men choose to read alone, others prefer to argue the point with friends. Read them, argue them, even use them to prop up your wobbly table in the lounge when you've finished. Either way, no Two Dogs man will ever say "I don't read books" as if it's a badge of honour.

Grrrr.

Two Dogs is published by SchreiberFord Publications and Struik.
info@twodogs.co.za
www.struik/twodogs.co.za

Published by Two Dogs
an imprint of SchreiberFord Publications and Struik Publishers

•

SchreiberFord Publications
PO Box 50664, The Waterfront, Cape Town, 8001

Struik Publishers
(a division of New Holland Publishing (South Africa) (Pty) Ltd)
PO Box 1144, Cape Town, 8000
New Holland Publishing is a member of Johnnic Communications Ltd

•

First published 2007

1 3 5 7 9 8 6 4 2

•

Publication © 2007 Two Dogs
Text © 2006 Rick Crosier, Andrew Donaldson, Daniel Ford, Tim Richman,
Josef Talotta, John Wardall

•

•

Publishing manager: Daniel Ford
Managing creative director: Grant Schreiber
Managing editor: Tim Richman
Designer: Gillian Stephens
Production manager: Valerie Kömmer

•

Reproduction by Hirt & Carter Cape (Pty) Ltd
Printed and bound by Paarl Print, Oosterland Street, Paarl, South Africa

•

ISBN 978-1-92013-715-1
info@twodogs.co.za
www.twodogs.co.za

That guy who let the dogs out…

ACKNOWLEDGMENTS

Sincere thanks go to the authors, Andrew, John, Josef, Rick and Tim, for contributing out of conviction – as South Africans and as writers – more than anything else. It's comforting to know that there are Saffers who have the opportunity to live abroad but choose to live here.

For South Africans, wherever you are

CONTENTS

INTRODUCTION: GOODBYE PERTHURBIA   11
Daniel Ford

WHY I'LL NEVER LIVE IN **THE UK** AGAIN   23
Andrew Donaldson

WHY I'LL NEVER LIVE IN **THE US** AGAIN   39
Josef Talotta

WHY I'LL NEVER LIVE IN **CANADA** AGAIN   55
John Wardall

WHY I'LL NEVER LIVE IN **OZ** AGAIN   73
Rick Crosier

WHY I'LL NEVER LIVE IN   97
NEW ZEALAND AGAIN
Tim Richman

GOODBYE
PERTHURBIA

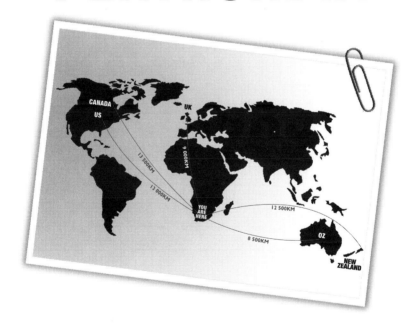

Hands up all those who've thought about emigrating. Oh yes, that includes you at the back pretending not to hear the question. Thank you.

A common talking point in South African daily life – whether it's dinner-party conversation, chatter around the office water cooler, serious talk with our partners late at night, or merely the voices in our heads – is the one about moving on. To a "better" country, a "safer" country, a country that offers our children "more opportunities". It happens everywhere and every day. At times, it seems to be a constant barrage. And while it might once have been an idea that was firmly associated with the privileged white population, the so-called chicken run, it's pretty well accepted now that the notion of moving on has more to do with money and skills: if you've got them, then you've got the luxury to consider emigrating; if you haven't, you're probably too concerned with the basics of finding a job and a house. But if you do have the means, then chances are you have at the very least *thought* about life in another country. In fact, I'd venture a guess that there isn't a person in this country who has the means to emigrate who hasn't at least pondered the idea of nice life in Perth or Sydney or Auckland or Toronto or wherever – Perthurbia, I like to call it.

There are, of course, the one-eyed patriots who tell us they're committed to South Africa forever and it's actually good that those who've chosen to leave have done just that. "The fewer people here in South Africa then the more opportunities for the rest of us," you're likely to hear.

Or they scoff at the idea of emigrating. "Who wants to live in a country where a dog shitting on a lawn makes front page news?" they might ask. "We're watching history in the making right around us in South Africa. It's boring everywhere else."

But all that reasoning like this tells us about the person spouting it is that they themselves have grappled with the thought of moving on; that they've made the decision to stay and need constant reassurance that it was the right one. They might even toss in a comment like, "Our friends Dave and Julie moved to London last year and you know what? Someone broke into their house the first week they were there and stole everything they owned." Somehow it diminishes our crime statistics in a flash. Our ever-transparent Ministry of Safety and Security would be proud.

And this constant justification is the exact opposite of what the ex-pats will argue once they've moved into their quiet home in suburban LA or Vancouver. Every time they're invited to a dinner party with locals, the topic will come up and they'll rattle off a recent horror story they picked up on the net or from phone calls back home, or they'll relate the latest economic figures (but only if the rand has just taken a hit). As with the South African who stays, the South African who goes wants to reassure himself – and everyone else – that he's made the right decision...

Every country has its share of people who move on to live elsewhere, looking for a new and different life, but there can't be many nations in the world as wealthy as ours where the possibility of emigration underscores daily life so emphatically. There are millions of Brits, Germans, Swiss and others who don't even contemplate leaving the country of their birth, while the few who do decide to ship off overseas are seen as modern-day adventurers. To us, the immovable people seem like boring stay-at-home types – they've probably never spent more than a week or two at a time overseas. But the mere fact that these types are in the majority provides a sense of stability in those societies that simply does not exist in our lives here. If a family moves to another country, it is a major event to them; for us, it may be disappointing to lose friends, but these things happen. All the time in fact. Meanwhile, it's unlikely that many Americans even know that other countries exist, let alone consider emigrating to them. But that's enough with the American bashing. At least until later in the book.

So why is it that South Africans seem to live in this constant state of flux, never sure which of our friends will be the next to announce that they're off "for the sake of the children", or indeed if the next people in our circle of friends to utter those words might be us? Why this constant idea of moving on?

Perhaps it's because we are a nation of immigrants ourselves – Europeans, Indians, other indigenous Africans. The Xhosas migrated down through southern African, the Afrikaners trekked into the unknown interior, the English arrived off the boats in the 1820s. There has always been social flux in our part of the world; perhaps we see moving and moving on as a logical extension of who we are and how we were created as a nation. It's natural. Unlike the Brits, Germans and Swiss mentioned earlier, who are bound to their countries by hundreds, perhaps thousands, of years of heritage, we all come from stock that has no special regard for remaining in one location.

South Africans also seem to consider success abroad to be that much worthier than success at home. We venerate locals who have made it overseas, like Charlize Theron or Dave Matthews or Gary Lubner of Autoglass or Brent Hoberman of lastminute.com, as proof of what Saffers can achieve in the "bigger" world, elevating them above those who have achieved the same levels of success at home. It's as if South Africans who've done well in England or America are winning in the premier league while the rest of us are still plodding along in the second division. We revel in the idea that there are hundreds of thousands of South Africans (more, according to Andrew Donaldson) taking over London/New York/ Sydney as further proof of how our nation can thrive anywhere it chooses. And, of course, even our president and many other of our political leaders were moulded outside of our borders. So who's to argue that moving on is a bad thing?

Our perceived isolation at the tip of Africa also drives many of us to seek out life "where it's happening", and probably explains why more young South Africans have been to Manchester than to Mooreesburg. New York-London-Paris remains the axis upon which the world seems to spin. You might add Berlin, Hong Kong, Sydney, LA to that list – but Cape Town and Johannesburg? Despite our country's current popularity among the Euro jet set, and some lame attempts from the fashion industry and the like to elevate us to that level, we'll never be that sophisticated – that "in".

The isolation reason is not unique to South Africa, as anyone who has spent time with the huge backpacking community of New Zealand, Australia and even Scandinavia will attest to. In fact, in 2001 it was estimated that nearly 15 per cent of people born in New Zealand were living outside the country of their birth. This perceived isolation will, for the foreseeable future, continue to drive people, especially young people in search of bigger, brighter things, to explore at length abroad. (Of course, an irony of Perth's vast SA ex-pat population is, as Rick Crosier mentions later, that it's considered to be the most isolated city in the world.)

As a note to the above, it is worth remembering that many of those who leave South Africa to live and work in other countries, particularly young people, don't leave with the intention of staying; rather, they are travelling to gain new experience, to "see the world" and to get themselves a financial head start – especially if they can do it earning pounds. Some of them end up staying, but those who return do so armed with new skills, and hopefully cash, which are injected into the country. This is to be applauded. (Except for the irritating habit of many a returnee who seems to think he was the first person to have visited London, and that serving pints "down the pub" for two years somehow endows him with a wealth of worldly knowledge – to be shared with all and sundry – and entitles him to a cushy job back home. To those people we say, please get over yourselves and humbly put your foot on the bottom rung of the career ladder.)

Of course, we cannot overlook the practical results of our recent past as a primary reason for leaving South Africa. The apartheid years saw a constant stream of locals packing up and shipping out to escape violence or persecution, or for moral reasons. And the former reason, as evidenced by our exceptionally high crime statistics, continues to drive emigration, or is at least *used* as the reason for leaving. Even if this reason is less significant than it was in the seventies and eighties, anecdotally at least, it does continue to provide a core justification for emigrants. But possibly not *the* core justification any more.

There is a strong current belief that many South Africans – of all races – are leaving our shores simply in search of better job prospects. Whether they are motivated by the perceived discrimination of affirmative action, the scarcity of jobs here or the notion of earning good money quickly, the research seems to suggest that foreign currency is the greatest lure these days. Just take a look at our rugby players if you still have doubts.

But enough with the reason *why* we leave. Just how many of us *are* leaving? Though the figures are notoriously inaccurate, because most emigrants don't advertise the fact to the relevant authorities, they all seem to suggest that our dinner party conversations are not just talk. According to the South African Migration Project (SAMP), 2003 saw 16,165 "self-declared" emigrants leave the country, the largest figure since the 1994 elections. At the extreme end of the scale, some estimates – admittedly disputed – suggest that a million South Africans have left our shores since then.

But – and here's the important but – after all the talk of emigration, the whys and wheres, the interesting trend these days, as reported by the international moving companies, seems to be that more and more South African are returning home to live. And they're flying in with an influx of foreign immigrants who have also heard about life at the bottom of Africa. Having arrived from the UK in 1994, I include myself on the last list. I'd visited South Africa and Zimbabwe several years earlier, and met a girl – now my wife – before making the move out here. To the absolute disbelief of the people heading the other way, I honestly felt Africa offered me more opportunities than England, and I haven't looked back.

So it was in early 2006 that I sat down over a beer with my managing editor, Tim Richman, who had recently returned from a year in Sydney to take up the job. We got to talking about life in Australia and he described his stay there as a memorable and amazing one. He couldn't recommend the city more. Thing is, it just wasn't Cape Town. It wasn't home. And for all their First World attractions and benefits, the Aussies have their share of problems that you just don't know about until you've lived among them for a while. He'd never intended on staying there forever, but he sure was glad to step off the plane in South Africa again. Just as I am every time I return from a trip back to the UK to visit friends and relatives.

Our conversation was not an isolated one. We'd both started hearing phrases like "Perth/London/Auckland is okay, but it's really not as good as South Africa", or similar sentiments, from people who had been there, done that and got the T-shirt. The more we heard the stories, the more it confirmed that not only is life not perfect in Perthurbia – washing up is washing up, no matter where you are – but, more importantly, life in South Africa is good. It's vibrant, it's exciting, it's real. And having a shop that sells boerewors and Mrs Balls half an hour's drive away just isn't the same.

The end result of our little chat is this book, *Why I'll Never Live In Oz Again*, which uses as its premise the fact that life is not always rosy in Perthurbia. It is written by South Africans who have lived in Australia, New Zealand, England, America and Canada, the five destinations most favoured by those leaving our shores seeking a new life. Three of them are natives, the other two are naturalised, but they all call themselves South Africans and they all call South Africa home (just as I do). If you'd heard that they had hated their times abroad and had failed to make a go of it, then you might be excused for being sceptical. But the truth is they were all successful outside of South Africa and, in fact, they quite enjoyed their time there. And contrary to our title, never doesn't really mean *never*; it's just that South Africa beats the pants off Perthurbia any day. So they packed up and shipped out again – to South Africa, to live where they really felt at home and happiest.

First up is Andrew Donaldson, who spent two years in London as a foreign correspondent for the *Sunday Times*. He has written a suitably eloquent piece that offers some surprisingly harsh words for a country veritably inundated with South Africans, and which still carries the dubious tag of "Mother Country" for many. Teen thuggery, Tony Blair and an ironic English bigotry all feature in his cross hairs. Despite these feelings, and though he feels that he could never live in London again, Andrew wouldn't mind "returning there now and then for a spot of shopping and taking in the odd gig at the Borderline".

Then, recent Mondi-winner Josef Talotta writes a series of letters to a fictional (but actually not-so-fictional) long-lost acquaintance: a South African who left for the US many years ago, around the same time he moved here. Appropriately, they capture a fantastic, almost American ebullience for his adopted country. There can't have been too many Americans immigrating to South Africa in the early nineties, but Josef was one of them, and our magazine industry (and the Johannesburg social scene) has been far better off for it. In one of the letters, he asks, "beyond family and friendships, what is life?" His answer is, "a series of places, events, moments, experiences and memories. And, in my opinion, South Africa delivers far more than most places…" I couldn't agree more.

England-born John Wardall spent 23 years living in Canada, and his montage of Canadian life is bone dry and spot on. He still has great admiration for the country where ice hockey is an obsession but, having married a South African and moved here fifteen years ago, he has found a more exciting home, where locals don't have to drive around frozen lakes, or fish through holes in them, for fun. Plus it's warmer here…

Then onto the title chapter, which is provided by Rick Crosier, who spent four years on and off living in Australia, a country that harbours much of his extended family. His piece is suitably Australian: bawdy, funny and telling it like it is. Rick spent most of his time in Brisbane and Melbourne: the former he likens to "Bellville with a different accent", while the latter is "the jewel in Australia's crown". So you can be assured of a subjective overview… or not.

Finally, we move on to New Zealand, where the rugby fans (which is to say everyone in the country, sheep included) are even more passionate and demanding than the nutjobs back home. Despite his recent year in Sydney, Tim Richman preferred to write this chapter, having lived in Auckland in 2000/2001, and having made the trip halfway around the world many times over the years to visit family. Though he has a fondness for the place that "has much to do with memories of my grandmother's Christmas pavlova and trout fishing with my grandfather on Lake Taupo", he believes that the country is only suitable for short holiday visits: "beyond that, you will go insane". Read his piece to discover what an amazing building the Auckland Sky Tower is – and why it is totally out of place in New Zealand.

So, if you are one of those people who has considered leaving South

Africa, read this book to remind yourself what a clever chap you are for staying. If you've been there and returned, read this book to remind yourself what a clever chap you are for coming back. And if you're still considering leaving, read this book for a reality check. And if you still insist on seeking out a place in Perthurbia, remember: the grass isn't always greener.

Daniel Ford
Two Dogs Publishing Manager

P.S. I am, ironically, writing this introduction while back in the UK. Just to reassure you, the weather hasn't got any better,

If Nature here wishes to make a mountain, she runs a range
for five hundred miles; if a plain, she levels eighty; if a rock,
she tilts five thousand feet of strata on end; our skies are
higher and more intensely blue; our waves larger than others;
our rivers fiercer. There is nothing measured, small nor petty
in South Africa.

– Olive Schreiner

A man travels the world over in search of what he needs
and returns home to find it.

– George Moore

WHY I'LL NEVER LIVE IN
THE UK AGAIN

BY ANDREW DONALDSON

Andrew Donaldson's Rosslyn Hill flat

AUTHOR PROFILE

Andrew Donaldson is a
senior journalist with the
Sunday Times. He lived
and worked in London
from 2004 to 2006 as a
correspondent for the
newspaper, but was happy to
return to Johannesburg, "the
world's most exciting city".
He was born in Cape Town,
and is quite fond of the idea
of holidays there.

> Why, Sir, you find no man, at all intellectual, who is willing to leave London. No, Sir, when a man is tired of London, he is tired of life; for there is in London all that life can afford.
>
> *Samuel Johnson*

One summer's evening, at the end of a long day with friends in Hertfordshire, I was dropped off at the station at Welwyn Garden City to catch a train back to London. Like the nearby towns of Stevenage and Hatfield, Welwyn Garden City is a relatively new settlement, slung up in the post-war years, and now popular with the Blairish super-middle classes; two-car families (one of them usually a sensible station wagon) who are prepared to put up with the grind of commuting to the office in London in return for what could be termed a suburban lifestyle in a clone town edged with a bit of country lushness. That is, the clusters of stand-alone three- and four-bedroomed houses have gardens, usually littered with dog turds and kids' toys, and there's a forest or park nearby with a pub around the corner which may or may not be called the something-or-other Arms.

Access to the station at Welwyn Garden City is through a shopping mall. On most days, the mall's parking lot is filled with commuters and shoppers' cars. However, given that this was a Sunday evening on a bank holiday weekend, it was now largely deserted, save for a group of about twenty or so teenaged boys and girls messing about near the mall's entrance. As I made my way across the car park it became clear that they were all quite drunk. I ignored them at first, but then one or two of them hurled insults my way – "Fat wanker!" – and they began walking over towards me.

This was a terrifying moment. Living in London, I had learned to fear English children. The newspapers and TV news programmes were full of stories of these feral monsters who roamed the housing estates in packs. Recently, a gay barman had been kicked to death by a group of kids, the oldest seventeen, as he made his way home along the South Bank. A fourteen-year-old member of that gang, barely literate, later wrote about it in her diary, describing the incident and the other attacks on passers-by that left them hospitalised that night. Elsewhere, a young South African, wearing a Springbok rugby jersey, was attacked by a gang of kids on bicycles as he and his two friends made their way home after watching a televised rugby match at a pub. He lost an eye. In another, more shocking incident of apparently random violence, a drunk man passed out at a bus-stop was doused with spirits and set alight by two eighteen-year-old thugs, who then filmed him with their cellphones as his clothing caught fire. Their victim survived the attack, but his injuries were considerable.

And so I was scared, fearing a beating at the hands of children in a deserted parking lot. But I pretended otherwise, and tried not to stare at them as I strode towards the mall's entrance. Then suddenly their attention dramatically shifted from me. One of the boys noticed his girlfriend – and here I'm presuming it was his girlfriend – kissing another boy, a full-on tongue-lashing-tonsil job, and they began screaming at one another. There were a few slaps, a lot of cursing and the sound of bottles smashing. I passed them and made it to the mall's entrance without looking back. The automatic doors slid open and shut behind me. As I turned a corner inside the mall, a security guard stepped out from behind a pillar where he had been hiding. "Are you okay, mate?" he asked. "They do anything to you out there?"

And here's a thing: the security staff at the mall had been watching this group on CCTV monitors. There is nothing unusual about this. The English are the most filmed society on the planet, with something like one camera for every seven or eight citizens. The grainy video clips of their drunken escapades in city centres invariably wind up on TV programmes about binge drinking and the debate over relaxing the country's arcane licencing laws; a grim montage of a shabby citizenry urinating, vomiting, brawling and fucking in gutters. Had I been attacked, it would have been recorded on video somewhere. Maybe even played out in court. After all, those two yobs who'd set the drunk man alight were caught thanks to surveillance cameras and hauled before the beak; the video clips from their phones, complete with horrifying soundtracks of the jokes they made as the flaming man writhed in agony and their brutal laughter, were played in court, and five will get you ten that this footage will soon be on television as well, part of some "documentary" on the sociology of inner-city violence. But, travelling back to London, I began to wonder: had I been attacked, would the security staff at the mall have intervened and come to my rescue? I had my doubts.

My attackers would have been children, and in England, children have been raised to fear no consequences of their actions. Teachers and parents fear *them*, and are prohibited, it seems, from taking disciplinary action against their wards. Here's the longish headline of an in-depth feature on violence in British schools from a May 2005 article in *The Independent On Sunday*: "A bully broke my daughter's nose. The injury nearly killed her – yet the school did nothing to stop the attacks". The opening sentences of the report: "It started with name-calling and ended with a vicious physical assault, two trips to hospital, a court case and a month off lessons. In between was a four-year campaign of classroom bullying against a girl whose only crime was to be well brought up." For four years, teachers at a Kent school were incapable of preventing a pupil from being attacked by her classmates? Sounds absurd, you'd think, but this kind of incident happens regularly all across the UK. Given reports that pupils carry guns and knives to school, you can hardly blame the staff for not wanting to get involved.

And if the kids are bad, wait until you have to deal with their parents. A new breed of parasite has emerged over recent years to leech off the welfare state: the so-called Neets, an acronym for those Not in Employment, Education or Training. These are the super-chavs, the breeders, according to the sociologists, of Britain's future criminal classes. In one celebrated case of Neet-ness, a woman in her thirties had, in order to be bumped up the welfare ladder and receive a larger council house and increased state benefits, encouraged her three daughters all to fall pregnant. Which they did. They were twelve, fourteen and sixteen years of age.

Modern England, I was finding, is a shit-hole. And it wasn't just the kids and their grubby parents, either. Pretty soon, the very nature of the political establishment, the class system, if you will, was starting to depress me. I'd arrived in February 2004 with a two-year contract as a London-based foreign correspondent for the *Sunday Times*. The salary was good and I soon stopped converting the sterling into rands. I lived in Holborn, around the corner from the British Museum. The flat was tiny by South African standards. When friends from Johannesburg stayed over, as they sometimes did, the blow-up mattress could barely fit into the sitting room. But Covent Garden and Soho were a few minutes away and for a while I thought that everything was perfect. The best bookshops in the world were nearby. The pubs in the area were grand old boozers and included the only bar in the city to still run a vinyl jukebox. The clubs and music haunts were ten minutes away. My life, it seemed, was good.

Pity, though, about the English elite. They really have got condescension down to a fine art. Well, not all of them. In fact, let's just say for the record that most of them are pretty decent folk, warm and generous to a fault. But there are a good few of them, weasel-hearted and mean-spirited, whose behaviour is so repulsive, so creepy, that it's hardly worth the effort distinguishing between good and bad. Chief culprit here is Tony Blair. It may seem unfair to judge people harshly merely because their prime minister is an oily berk who went to war on the say-so of a doltish American imperialist, but hey, they elected him, this neo-Thatcherite shit. And then returned him to office. Twice.

You've seen Blair on television countless times. But it's only when you're in the same room as him, at press conferences, trying to get him to take your questions that you realise how loathsome he is. His press briefings at Downing Street that I attended were extraordinary exercises in contempt for journalists and our work. Questions about the unfolding catastrophe in Iraq were invariably fobbed off, with dismissive responses that began, "Well now, I think if you really listened to the case for war you'd find blah blah blah" – meaning, "You don't really understand this, what I'm trying to do here, do you? That's because you're stupid."

Then there was all that rubbish about "the scar of Africa", about healing the world. "Yes," said Blair, "we've all had a chat about it, the leaders of the G8 countries and I, and, well, we've agreed that we're all against African poverty. Certainly, we've had to think about lifting trade barriers and restrictions, and we've had to think about debt cancellation, and we've had to think about aid and how to stop children dying. And gosh, there's a lot of that, thinking about children dying. We've had to do that. We've had to think about all that. Well, we've had to think about doing that by 2010. Certainly, by then, by 2010, we will have thought about all that, maybe even a lot more than you'd imagine…"

Well, it was kinda nice putting us on the agenda like that, making the continent the theme of Britain's presidency of the G8, but one big reason Africa has scars in the first place is because British arms manufacturers do such good business here. That's how Blair's foreign policies "heal" Africa, by selling its ratbag leaders guns with which to kill their political opponents. And then he thinks drinking mugs of tea at press conferences makes him look "matey" and "blokey". It doesn't. It reinforces the conviction that here we have a Grade-A twat of a world leader.

Which shouldn't bother me in the slightest. At the time of writing, Blair was reckoned to be on the way out, and the chancellor, Gordon Brown, waiting to take his place. Incidentally, Brown also thinks something has to be done about Africa. But let's not hold our breath; it was in Kenya, during his first trip to the continent, that he dared suggest that colonialism had not been such a bad thing. No, really. Brown said that. I don't know what he was thinking, but we can hazard a guess, and it is this: the British – unlike, let's say, the Belgians – did infrastructural stuff in Africa, built roads and hospitals, gave these poor savages administrations and schools, lasting and permanent things. How can that be bad? Reading and writing? I don't know what the Kenyans thought of this, but again, we can hazard a guess: this British empire, which hanged so many Kenyans during the Mau Mau rebellions, a good thing? Not on this side of the fence.

Consider the theme of the fancy-dress party that Prince Harry attended dressed as a Nazi a mere fortnight before memorial ceremonies across Europe commemorated the liberation of Auschwitz: "Colonials and Natives". Excuse me, but how weird is that? Who has "Colonials and Natives" parties? Do you know anyone who has been to a "Colonials and Natives" party? No?

Actually, the Royal family are quite fond of throwing colonial-themed bashes. The 2003 party at Windsor that was so memorably gate-crashed by the British prankster Aaron Barshak was also a "Colonial" job. Empire remains important to these people, for all the wrong reasons.

And this goes to the heart of why I couldn't ever settle in England. I am, I suppose, a "colonial", a South African. I need to know my place, and, whenever I stray and drift off the plan, I need to be put back there with a stern reminder that, indeed, that is where I belong. And, as a South African colonial, I should realise that I am not really even the same sort of colonial as those nice chaps from Australia and New Zealand. No, I am a pig-shit thick racist.

This is how David Quantick, journalist and alleged humorist, describes South Africans, in his book *Grumpy Old Men On Holiday* (HarperCollins):

> Known among backpackers as "the nation that used to pretend it was someone else on holiday". Until the release of Nelson Mandela from his long incarceration, South Africans were the holiday scum of Europe, pariahs of inter-railing. With their strange accents, part Dutch, part Cyberman, they were easy to spot. Their curious attitude to racial matters preceded them, but their apparent belief that some peoples were inferior to others was agreed on by all, although it was the South Africans everyone felt were the inferior ones. Soon you would hear South Africans claiming that they were in fact from New Zealand or some nicer country, just to have someone to talk to.
>
> Nowadays, of course, all South Africans despise racism and they are among the most liberal of rich, white, privileged tourists.

Quantick's apparent belief that all South Africans are stupid white Afrikaners is neither here nor there, but as a white South African who has lived in London for two years, I can confirm that he is not alone in his bigotry. Most South Africans in England will be familiar with the snide and condescending put-down that goes something like this: "Oh, you're from South Africa! Gosh, another South African over here! So many of you! Why did you all leave? Can't stand living under a black government?" (Cab-drivers will add a helpful "Can't say I blame you" just to be extra insulting.)

But the weird thing is that you can understand and almost forgive the English for their antipathy towards South Africans. There are a shit-load of us out there, happily living London and holding down steady jobs. In 2004, I attended a "friendship" ceremony at City Hall, where Johannesburg mayor Amos Masondo and his London counterpart and host, Ken Livingstone, signed an agreement stating that the two cities would be chums. What struck me about that evening, apart from his using the occasion to bash the British National Party, was Livingstone's apparent belief that the South African population in London was little more than five thousand. A source at the South African High Commission suggested rather that, conservatively, there were more than a million in the capital. Not for nothing are the south-western boroughs of London now referred to as Wimblefontein.

Which didn't mean there was a South African community in London or, indeed, the country. It just meant there were lots of South Africans. Lots and lots of them, all different to one another – young, old, black, white, gay, straight, English-speaking, Afrikaans – and I went out of my way to have as little as possible to do with them. If I needed to hang around South Africans, well, what was the point of coming to London? But, occasionally, I would meet up with my countrymen. Some would be decent folk, others you'd flee from in horror. Ordinarily, I stayed well away from the Walkabout chain of pubs or the Bok Bar in Covent Garden, regular Saffer drinking spots, especially on match days. The Walkabout is an Australian chain, derided by English trendies as being the haunt of antipodeans too bone-brained to get to grips with the local culture (ten pints of piss ale, a bag of pork scratchings and an upchuck on the way home), but most of its customers are Saffers. When the Springboks play, Walkabouts across England are stuffed with drunk oafs in green and gold jerseys, often loudly singing *Die Stem*, as if the last half-century hadn't happened.

I once chatted to three of them, all rugby fans in their early twenties, over beers in a quiet pub on the Clerkenwell Road with a view to writing a feature on Saffers at large in the big overseas. It was a dire experience. Their views appalled me, and I killed the story. They were from Kroonstad and they hated everything about the UK. They especially hated the English. Surely, I pressed them, there was something about living in London that was good, something enjoyable, else why stay? They thought hard. Yes, there was. They liked fucking girls from Eastern Europe. They knew, they said, some beautiful women from Latvia and Poland who apparently opened their legs at the drop of a hat. Only problem, they added, these girls were "thicker than kaffirs" and struggled to "talk good English". We're talking about some seriously retarded thinking here. The good news, I suppose, is that Kroonstad's finest are over there – and maybe that's where they will stay, raising a family with some unfortunate Latvian girl in a nasty flat over a chip shop in Elephant and Castle. But I wouldn't count on it. Those Eastern European girls, they're getting smarter all the time.

But a perhaps more pitiful group of South Africans are those professionals who arrived in England in the eighties, fleeing the madness of PW Botha's rule. Now forty- or fiftysomething, they've just become too established, too settled, to return. They'd really like to, honestly, but, you know, the kids, well, they're at school here and they've got friends, and who's going to employ middle-aged white people back home, hey, but we do like to get back now and then for a holiday, visit some relatives… so it goes. I met a lot of them in Hampstead, where I shared a home with a friend in 2005.

Hampstead, it must be said, was an agreeable and rather gentrified neck of the woods. Our two-storeyed flat, in a row of terraced houses on Rosslyn Hill, was large and comfortable. Weekends were happy there, the high street buzzed, and for a while I began to feel part of a community. But living in Hampstead meant commuting to work on the Northern Line, arguably the worst of the Underground systems. Trains were always crowded, jammed with irritable commuters. They were forever late and broke down often. In summer, Transport for London advised commuters, especially those on the Northern Line, that they should shower in the morning before going to work because, given the Stygian hell down there, the odour of unwashed armpits would be too overpowering. I wrote a short piece about this and my other commuting experiences. Some readers back home were quite angry with me. They were, I suspect, the sort who still harboured strong feelings for the "Mother Country". One man fumed that he had visited London only recently and, although he didn't use the Northern Line, he found that he had to wait no more than three minutes for his train. Further, he asked, what was the problem with a little body odour? Was I some sort of sissy? Had I ever travelled on the Paris Metro with all those garlic eaters? And what about the buses in Africa? Had I been on one of those smelly journeys? Where they have goats and chickens on the seat next to you?

Goats and chickens? On a bus ride in Africa? I thought of this on a bitterly cold winter's day in Camden towards the end of my time in London. It was dark, the sky was grey and so low that it seemed as if it would crush the city. My hands were curled into fists in the pockets of my overcoat. I suddenly had a vision of myself in a bus on a hot day, somewhere in Africa, rolling down a rutted country road. The windows were open and there was a warm breeze in my face. The goat next to me had peed on the floor. The chickens didn't like it, but all I could smell was ripe fruit in the baskets and cardboard boxes on the racks overhead. I couldn't wait to get back home.

England is nothing but the last ward of the European madhouse, and quite possibly it will prove to be the ward for particularly violent cases.

– Leon Trotsky

Oh England is a pleasant place for them that's rich and high,
But England is a cruel place for such poor folks as I.

– Charles Kingsley

Never again will I spend another winter in this accursed
bucketshop of a refrigerator called England.

– Rudyard Kipling

$

WHY I'LL NEVER LIVE IN
THE US AGAIN

BY JOSEF TALOTTA

The Talotta house in suburban Baltimore

AUTHOR PROFILE

Josef Talotta is a
Johannesburg-based lifestyle
brand consultant, writer
and Mondi Award-winning
columnist. He was born
in Cleveland, Ohio – "the
Bloemfontein of the States"
– and raised in Maryland,
though his European parents
and widespread family always
provided him with a "global
outlook". He moved to
South Africa in 1992.

My dearest Mandy

I can't believe it, but next week is 21 years since we met in Umhlanga in 1986! Our friendship has officially come of age! Whoever would have thought? It's funny how life works out. To think this innocent little American varsity boy would land up living in Johannesburg of all places, while such an über-Joburg chick like you has since become an American. Maybe we're cultural swap-outs? Although, you've gotta admit, dear Mandy, it was rather unfair of you to egg me on with "Move to SA! It's amazing!" right there in the middle of a State of Emergency and then to jump ship a few years before the change of government! And, what's more, I can't believe you've never been back – not even for a visit!

Well, next month also marks my 15th anniversary of arriving in sunny SA. A lot has happened since 1992, both personally and in my adopted country. You might find it hard to believe, but life here – in spite of some white middle-class perceptions – has improved a million times over. You wouldn't recognise the country! For starters, Joburg has literally burst its borders and been super-sized – land-wise it's even bigger than Los Angeles. The city's borders have spread to Pretoria's southern suburbs now and include Midrand, which has since expanded to connect the two cities into one metropolitan area. Pretoria is no longer lazy-dozy and has also boomed, with something like 30,000 diplomats running around. You wouldn't recognise Parkhurst, either. Remember that staid old suburb adjacent to Victory Park, where you grew up? Well, its high street is now lined with restaurants, coffee bars and chi-chi little boutiques selling everything from antiques to bits from Tiffany's. I kid you not. Even the airport – which you knew as Jan Smuts, before it had a ten-year stint as Joburg International and is now trading as OR Tambo – has expanded. Then again, it had to. We have a million new low-cost airlines now, so you can fly to Cape Town for $100 return, not to mention a gazillion new international carriers coming in from all over. Times have changed since the "daze" of SAA/SAL and the dozen-odd sanctions-busting carriers from the mid-'80s.

Shopping-wise, you'd love Joburg these days. Okay, not that it offers anything you wouldn't find in the States – well, I suppose we have our own "Proudly South African" home-grown designers – but the point is your old stomping ground, Sandton City, has been refurbished a few times since you left and could be right out of suburban Atlanta (very Buckhead indeed), complete with Louis Vuitton, Gucci, Mango, Timberland, Diesel, Häagen-Dazs, McDonald's, you name it. As a rule, suburban South African women still dress up to go shopping, even for groceries. Full war paint, the works! No sloppy tracksuits with running shoes like you see in the States. At the very worst, they'll do "designer sweats" with Puma takkies – think Kate Moss rather than Roseanne Barr – but only with huge wraparound sunglasses.

Of course, that's the point, isn't it? We still make an effort here. Yes, we have fast food here, but it's generally served on plates, with crockery and table service. And what's wrong with eating like that? If you ask me, fast food doesn't mean it has to be wrapped in paper, cardboard and polystyrene... Yes, McDonald's (and Wendy's and Burger King, etc) have their place – but I don't think the middle class here will ever really turn to them as a source of daily sustenance like in the States. No super-sizing here. Don't forget, just because it's cheap today doesn't mean it's cheap tomorrow. I think far too many Americans only need look in the mirror to see what super-sizing really means!

Bimbos is still going strong, but it's been rounded out by great South African chains like Nando's peri-peri chicken – lekker, lekker, lekker! – which is no doubt why it's rightfully become a global phenomenon, although not quite ready to take on the States. I can hear you cackling. Don't laugh too hard too soon! With the exception of McDonald's (which takes credit cards here!), South African consumers have pretty much rejected most American attempts to enter the fast food market. TGI-Friday's, Domino's Pizza and Chic-Fil-A have all come and gone. Not sure what happened to TGIF or Chic-Fil-A, but I think Domino's didn't anticipate the quality of South African pizza, which is more Italian (thin-crust) in flavour and prepared in wood-burning ovens – what you call "gourmet pizza" in your neck of the woods is our everyday corner-store pizza made by real off-the-airplane Italians nogal. Besides, we have our own home-grown pizza brands like St Elmo's, Scooters and Debonairs, all of which do home delivery, the latter in a tuxedo! Burger-wise, I think you must know it's Steers – and not McDonald's – that wins "best burger" in the Best of Johannesburg Peoples' Choice awards every single year.

Right. I don't know if you were in the mood for an SA-since-1994 update but that seems to have been my spiel. Otherwise, all's well. What's news on your end? Do you have an American accent yet? Mine's become somewhat South African in its own weird way. Tell me everything!

Love
Josef

My dearest Mandy

I knew you'd mention it! Crime schmime... Yes, yes, crime *is* a problem and I'd be lying if I said I haven't been affected by it. But I think you need to keep things in perspective. Remember your State of Emergency chant throughout the 1980s when you were travelling? "South Africa isn't as bad as you think and it's a very complex country," you'd say. What was your favourite comeback? Something like, "I mean, it's not as if there are bombs going off in my living room!" I think crime's similar. It has become the national obsession – which is a good thing. But, again, it stems from very complex factors and we are able – for the most part – to go about our daily lives. No, I don't stroll around Hillbrow with a Rolex, but then again, I never did in Baltimore, Washington or New York. I dare say I have a head-start on the security vibe, having lived in inner cities in the States. The difference here is that we suburban South Africans need to apply urban survival skills like your downtown DC, Baltimore and Philadelphia counterparts. It's weird, but it works.

For example, I live in a Sandton "cluster complex", which weren't really here in your time; they're what you call "gated communities" in the States (I must say, I was surprised to read of their ascent there). Of course, once you're "in" a complex, you're "out" of it for the most part – as close to emigration as one might get without leaving the country! The bottom line? Joburg – "crime capital of the world" – ironically has a statistically lower murder rate than Washington DC, where I lived throughout the '80s (without a problem, mind you).

You also asked about downtown Joburg being a no-go zone. Not so. The CBD – all 18 square kilometres of it – is divided into City Improvement Districts; some are okay, some are brilliant and *some* are no-go. The Financial District, near the Rand Club (yes, it's still going), is spotless, and countless buildings are being snapped up and renovated into luxury apartments. It's this part of town that offers the most promise, and which will drive the city centre's regeneration.

I dare say, Mandy, these initiatives are part of South Africa's can-do spirit, much of it driven by younger people who see themselves as drivers (and not passengers) of the country's future. I'm nursing a bit of a babalas as I write, as just last night I was jolling at Michy Lissoos's annual NOAH (Nurturing Orphans of Aids for Humanity) bash. It was at Summer Place in Hyde Park (the old Chiavelli home). It was great – you would've loved it! Around 120 punters who each paid R250 to attend (money to NOAH) – and we pulled in more than R30,000 just jolling. Summer Place donated the venue, Arnold Tanzer (local celeb caterer) from Food On The Move pitched in some free food, a really hot Joburg mobile bar company, LiquidChefs, did free welcome drinks and all our friends' companies donated free lucky draw prizes. All we did was laugh, dance (courtesy of DJ Goldilocks who plays the infamous annual Gemini bash), smoke and yak. Just up your alley! There are so many of these charity drinks bashes going on these days – the monthly Thursday Club in Joburg, the East Rand and Cape Town (nearly a million rand to Starfish, another brilliant AIDS charity); and I'm involved with the Veuve Clicquot MediaSalon, a monthly charity drinks mixer at the swank Peech hotel in Melrose. There are so many interesting, exciting things on the go here, all being set up and run by young movers and shakers who are hungry for success *and* fun at the same time.

By contrast when I visit the States every year, all I hear are people talking about TV shows, leaf-blowers, new sneaker ranges and the latest technology. Americans are sweet enough but – with geographical distance and mental hindsight – I dare say far too many come across as overgrown children. Then again, it's a very insular and inward-looking country as expected, considering less than 20% of your fellow countrymen have passports! Still globally naïve…

Sorry, don't mean to take a swipe at your adopted country – not forgetting it's where I was born!

Best I sign off before I get into trouble.

Baci di Africa
Josef
xoxo

Mands!

Thanks for your missive. A bit harsh, gotta say, even though I expected it.

Yes, you are correct – the majority of South Africans don't have passports either but let's look at incomes, shall we? From what I've read, only around 17% of Americans have passports, but you know very well more than 17% of the US population *can* afford to travel overseas. I think you'd find the majority of the South African middle class does have a passport – and many use them. Big difference. In fact, that's the fundamental difference!

Your memories of South Africa seem stuck around 1987, that of an isolated pariah at the bottom of the African continent. Knowing both the US and SA rather intimately, I can name a number of areas where South Africa leaves the States behind. I mean, beyond family and friendships, what is life? It's a series of places, events, moments, experiences and memories. And, in my opinion, South Africa delivers far more than most countries.

For example, supermarkets are far better here for many reasons.

You are right, we don't have 38 types of chocolate chip cookies to choose from, but are you conveniently forgetting that 35 of your choices are uninspired tasteless kak made by an industrial foods conglomerate in New Jersey? Dairy products here – particularly yoghurts – are a thousand times better; our fruit and vegetables are not as large and shiny (and sinister, me thinks) as their American counterparts, but they certainly taste better. And importantly, our supermarkets are in local shopping malls, which makes far better sense as far as errand-running goes. Speaking of which, our malls can give US malls a run for their money any ol'day. They're generally cleaner, more visually up-to-date and with far better natural finishes like granite and marble. Our cinema chains, too, are of better standard: cleaner, more lux and with reserved seating. There's something uncivilised about just rocking up and plopping down at the movies, as you do in the States; I mean, it's not a rock concert! It's the little touches and finishes that count most in the daily grind, if you ask me.

Speaking of finishes, you quite simply can't compare a South African suburban house to its American counterpart. Ours are solid brick and plaster – old-style – and not prefab cardboard throw-togethers built en masse. The only upside to American homes is that I immediately know where the guest loo is – from coast to coast – as it's always under the stairs, just off the entrance hall. I don't think I ever heard an American ask, "Excuse me, where's the guest bathroom?" Don't you find that just a bit creepy? Very *Truman Show*…

Mandy, you mustn't confuse quantity with quality – a rather quaint American trait. To borrow a phrase from Isherwood, you sound like a dreary French intellectual arriving in the colonies for the first time, circa 1785. I mean, globalisation – *hello*! Do you really think we're still stuck in a time warp, only reading *Fair Lady* and *Scope*? In the past ten years, pretty much every single international mag title has launched a South African edition. Condé Nast mags has set up shop here, so there are local editions of *House & Garden*, *GQ* and *Glamour*, along with new SA editions of *marie claire*, *Elle*, *FHM*, *Men's Health*, *Shape*, *InStyle*, *Time Out*, etc. *GQ* and the other men's mags mean your chances of seeing a safari shorts set, with comb-in-sock and moustache, are near impossible these days. Shame, those kinds of okes are pretty much an endangered species, along with slap chips and Lion Lager.

Which brings me to my next point… They often get it completely wrong but, clothing-wise, South Africans make so much more of an effort than their American counterparts. They're far less slapgat in their weekend run-around gear – it's still very much a smart-casual kind of country, along with good manners for children and orderly queues. I can't believe how brat-like so many American children are, missing the basic fundamentals like "please" and "thank you" – not that I like being called "sir" or "Oom", mind you! A bit too young for that!

Cinnabon just opened in Sandton last week (its melted sugar ensures the entire banking hall now smells like an American mall which, I dare say, is the scent of pending obesity) and rumour has it that Starbucks will be making its South African debut this year. All that's really missing is the GAP (very '90s), Tower Records, H&M and IKEA and we're pretty much done – although I know the Virgin Megastores chain is also sniffing round the local market. I guess what I'm saying is globalisation ensures we pretty much have whatever you have – with the bush thrown in for dessert! (Please note, that's "the bush"– not "Bush"! See how well-behaved I've been steering clear of *that* topic?)

Gotta fly. You really should visit and see for yourself!

Love
Josef

Dear Mandy

Interesting point you've made about not really making great friends like you had here in the 15-plus years you've been in the States. Like South Africans, Americans are very friendly but I always experienced that more on a surface level – things seemed to fall apart on the follow-through. I'm not sure what it is. Maybe it's just the schlep of entertaining at home. Of course, it does make a huge difference by having domestic "help" at home, which means, unlike Americans, we don't have to use paper plates when we have a braai! (Again, detail is everything…) But there's more to it. There's something in the South African psyche that ensures an effort is made – whether it's collecting visitors from the airport (note how in London or New York, the visitor always has to fend for himself when arriving) or heating plates before serving dinner. Maybe it's my European heritage coming to the fore, but I like all these little personal details that are so lacking in the States. I like the fact that a little extra grunt goes into living – Americans tend to look for convenience but, you know what? Guests, dinner parties, entertaining and socialising aren't always convenient. My thinking? If someone is going to make an effort to invite me to a braai – to host me – then he or she can offer more than a hot dog and a plop of potato salad on a paper plate. I don't think Americans are mean-spirited (in fact, I think – along with Australians – they're probably the most psychologically similar to suburban South Africans); I just think they're time-poor, which makes them cut corners when it comes to quality. South Africans simply have more European-style flair and tend to follow "old school" rules when it comes to entertaining.

I also think – with TV coming so late here – that South Africans are much less legends in their own minds and less apt to speak out than their American counterparts. This swings two ways. On one hand, a famous actor or actress can stroll through Cape Town's Waterfront and, while people may twitter, chances are no-one's gonna scream out American-style, "Yo! Charlize, how ya doin', babe?" On the other hand, no-one here will get involved if a parent smacks a child's bum in a supermarket. Try that in the States! You're living in a society raised on TV and in front of video machines – Americans are very camera savvy and not afraid to speak their mind. Exhibit A: reality TV. Of course, this can backfire. Not everyone can be Paris Hilton. And there's the rub. Maybe they're simply too busy living TV lives to be real? After all, if they've created their own life show where they're the star (wardrobe by Abercrombie & Fitch), why should they invite you to guest star on it? Maybe they simply think you should organise your own show?

I don't know, Mandy. I sometimes think there are just too many screens in the States: TV screens, computer screens, PlayStation screens, LED screens, cellphone screens, directional and mini-TV screens in cars… It's almost like the more screens there are, the less real the people become. Even your national disasters – like the war in Iraq or 9/11 or Hurricane Katrina – are played out on screens. A lot of money goes into those screens, but what kind of quality of life do you really, truly get out at the end of it all? I can only compare that to South African story-telling at the tail-end of a braai. A space where people connect – with eye contact, touch, laughter and spirit – as humans. It might not be filmed with a mini hand-held camcorder, but it's real.

Ultimately, I think that's the difference between the two countries. The US is a slick, multi-million dollar film and South Africa is a theatrical stage production. The movie's special effects are impressive, but shortlived in your memory – and the audience need not participate on an invested level. They just sit back and enjoy the ride. It's bigger, but more watered down. With theatre, you need to engage your brain and bring your imagination to the production as an active participant. It's smaller, but more intense.

Perhaps that's why I'm so happy here. I've always preferred stage work over movies. And maybe that's why you feel a bit lost on that end? Growing up with a theatre life, you probably thought the movie world might offer so much more and are a bit disappointed now that you're living it? Think about it. Carry the analogy through: at movies, you have Coke and popcorn; at theatre you have coffee (or a whisky, if you're clever). Coke gives you a sugar rush; it's great at the time, until your sugar level drops. The only way to raise it up again is to have another Coke. And round and round it goes. To me, that's life in America. A big, never-ending can of Coca-Cola. No wonder you're always exhausted!

You need to learn how to replicate a long, lazy South African Sunday again – I fear you've forgotten how to chill. And how to live.

All my best
Josef
x

American society is a sort of flat, fresh-water pond
which absorbs silently, without reaction, anything which
is thrown into it.

– Henry B Adams

America has never quite grasped
that you can live in a place without making it ugly,
that beauty doesn't have to be confined behind fences,
as if a national park were a sort of zoo for nature.

– Bill Bryson

America is dumb. It's like a dumb puppy that has big teeth
that can bite and hurt you; aggressive. My daughter is four,
my boy is one. I'd like them to see America as a toy, a broken
toy. Investigate it a little, check it out, get this feeling and
then get out.

– Johnny Depp

WHY I'LL NEVER LIVE IN
CANADA AGAIN

BY JOHN WARDALL

The Wardalls' "Canadian dream" country cottage.

AUTHOR PROFILE

John Wardall was born in
Chester in England. He
moved to Toronto in 1967,
where he wrote for *The
Globe And Mail*, *Financial Post*,
Maclean's and a variety of
business publications. He
became group publisher and
editorial director at Canada's
largest publishing company,
before moving to Cape Town
with his South African wife
in 1992.

In 1936, the stalwart Mountie Sergeant Bruce, played by Nelson Eddy, resplendent in red coat and boy scout hat, singing *Rose-Marie* to Jeanette MacDonald and gazing lovingly at his horse, set the scene for the popular world view of Canada – even though the movie was shot in California. *Rose-Marie* may have been filmed seventy years ago, but the Canadian identity that it projected has been more enduring and influential than anything John Wayne ever did for America.

Today, poor old Nelson looks a bit fruity in the flickering, scratchy black-and-white talkie, but that is the result of passing time and changing style rather than the continuing belief that Canada remains much the same. A spoof movie, *Dudley Do-Right* – Dudley being the bumbling Mountie – was made in 1999 as a take-off of *Rose-Marie*, and showed just how the staid, good-guy image continues. Together, the movies encapsulate how reality has changed, though perception has not. The coats and horseflesh only come out of mothballs on ceremonial occasions for the tourists' cameras; the rest of the time, the Mounties chase their villains in Chevrolets and brown jackets.

Staid, good, honest, simple, ethical, law-abiding, nice, white, bland and cold sums up the typical picture the world supposes of Canada. In one simple word, it can probably be summed up as boring. Oh dear, the world is doing what it universally condemns as politically incorrect: it is stereotyping. And the stereotype, as it usually is, is both right and wrong.

Certainly most accepted norms are vastly different from those in South Africa. Canadians generally live a life free of many of the social pressures faced by South Africans, where people in all sectors live in a narrow comfort zone, regardless of their wealth, education or position in the pecking order.

There is an edge to living in South Africa that simply doesn't exist in Canada. Comparative newspaper headlines are interplanetary in their distance apart. A story that appeared on the front page of a major newspaper's regional section during my last visit to Toronto almost farcically illustrates this difference.

A stop sign on a quiet side street in a sleepy suburb had become partly obscured by an overhanging branch; a concerned citizen had telephoned the local municipal offices to warn the authorities of this danger; immediately, emergency procedures sprang into action... The story went on to describe how a police car was dispatched to monitor the intersection until the threat was removed. That was followed in short order by a city works crew, which removed enough of the offending branch as necessary while taking due care not to damage the tree. The tree-huggers were happy, endangered motorists were happy and concerned local residents could sleep safely in their beds once again. From telephone call to resolution took 45 minutes, meeting the targeted response time set by the accountable departments. If you live in Canada, this is front-page drama – with the predictable happy ending.

Everything in Canada is very civilised and really as it should be. Canadians certainly know how to behave. Come to a full stop at a stop sign. Do not jaywalk, or a lurking policeman will instantly produce a summons. Make sure you carry a full set of replacement bulbs in your car because, if a rear light blows and you're driving to get a replacement, it's already too late. Lose points for speeding and you're on your way to losing your licence. And pray the postman doesn't slip on your front path or you could be in for thousands of dollars in compensation. Warning signs are everywhere, advising sightseers to stay away from the edge or drivers to be on the lookout for wandering moose. (Not a bad idea, actually, as every year the odd complacent driver dies after ploughing into one of the great-horned beasts.)

It all sounds a bit much of a nanny state to most South Africans, who live in a much more undisciplined, unprotected, unstructured and under-enforced condition. But Canadians like it that way and, having lived there for 23 years, I've got to admit that it has much going for it. You don't walk out of your front door in the morning or return home at night wondering if you're going to get hijacked, robbed, raped or murdered. Those are rare occurrences in Canada.

But Canadians don't just like it that way (and frankly who wouldn't in that respect); they also expect and insist that government takes responsibility at all levels for protecting them from themselves. Another story illustrates this perfectly – this one, with a not-so-happy ending, taking place in Toronto after two teenaged boys had been given quad bikes for Christmas.

The boys lived near an open piece of land owned by the city. The hilly plot had been securely fenced and had no-trespassing and warning signs all around the perimeter. Nonetheless, the boys were determined to enjoy their new gifts to the full and, in very un-Canadian fashion, broke down the fence and proceeded to race each other on the notoriously unstable vehicles up and down the hills. Inevitably, they crashed into each other: one boy died, the other was paralysed. There was outrage that the youngsters had been able to break through the fence: the whole horrific incident was quite obviously the city's fault, and the ensuing lawsuit resulted in the city paying millions of dollars of compensation to the boys' parents. Mind-boggling, I know. And you will search to the end of your days to find a similar tale in South Africa. Our local governments struggle to protect their citizens from each other, let alone themselves.

On the recreational front, excitement in Canada can be found in almost anything. Maybe that's why Canadians are so content. I came to realise this after an invitation to go ice-fishing, a popular winter pastime.

Rising at four o'clock on a bitterly cold winter morning, dark outside, wind blowing and mounds of frozen snow lining the street, I bundled up in long-johns, multiple layers of clothing, a sheepskin coat and a woolly ski toque pulled down well over the ears. It was basic survival kit for the conditions. The noisy arrival of the culprits who talked me into this, in a massive 4x4, air horns blasting the neighbours awake, was the start of a truly dreadful day.

We shimmied and slid about one hundred kilometres north of the city into pristine, white countryside, arriving finally on the shores of a frozen lake as big as Gauteng. Far in the distance in the middle of the lake were a dozen tiny huts, separated from each other by no more than fifty metres. The operator of this sporting facility ushered his four most recent victims onto a toboggan and towed us by snowmobile, eyes squinting to avoid the driving sleet, out to one of the huts. Inside was a small paraffin heater and a couple of hard wooden benches on either side of the main attraction – yup, you guessed it – a hole in the ice.

For the next six hours, we sat, hunched over on the benches, drinking beer and staring at the fishing lines, which descended through the hole and did not so much as twitch for the duration of our vigil. Hadn't had so much fun since Granny's funeral.

When our host arrived to drag us back to sanity, he professed himself pleased to see we were all still there. Still there? Where on earth would we go without freezing to death? Ah, but that was the point, said he...

Earlier in the winter, he had taken a group of eight out to two huts. After consuming copious amounts of hooch, no doubt attempting to numb the brain to its surroundings – it worked – one of the intrepid adventurers decided to startle his colleagues in the next hut by taking off his clothes, descending down his hole into the water and swimming under the ice to emerge up through their hole. He partially achieved his aim by descending into the depths – and he certainly startled his colleagues when they all realised what he'd done – but, to no surprise of the alcoholically deprived, he did not appear at the next hut and, at last report, his frozen remains have yet to be found. No doubt the fish, which have a clear aversion to bait, found his pickled brain far more to their taste.

And so we see what a Canadian winter can drive a man to do...

There is no denying the beauty of the countryside after a heavy snowfall. Unlike the city, where it all quickly turns to brown slush from passing cars, the pristine white panorama of the countryside can be quite spectacular. So, it did not take long after the fishing fiasco for me to be persuaded to take a drive out to the country to witness a car race on ice. Oh yes, the unwary foreigner is a sucker for the new and exotic experience.

Here's what the maniac ice-racers do: they put tyres with metal studs in them on their cars and career around an oval race track marked out in the middle of a frozen lake (yes, another one; there are lots of lakes in Canada, and most of them freeze over in winter). If it sounds quite exciting, believe me when I tell you you'll get more of a high watching paint dry – fumes or no fumes.

After the racing was over, spectators drove their own cars out onto the ice to slither and slide and generally have a whale of a time. Not to be outdone, I – brain also in neutral – followed the lead of the whooping would-be boy-racers. There were too many cars near the edge, so I followed a bright red Dodge Charger with twenty-inch wheels and about eight exhaust pipes out towards the middle of the lake. It's hard to fathom why you're always surprised when these things happen but, suddenly, the rear of the car tipped upwards and I had myself a perfect view of its petrol tank. The front of the Charger had gone through the ice and the car was now slowly sliding under.

I would have been frozen by fear more than the temperature, I'm sure, but the young couple inside smashed the rear window with a wrench, clambered across the boot and ran back towards my car. Within a couple of minutes, the shiny muscle car, their pride and joy, had slid quietly beneath the ice.

Whatever conditions you live in, you have to make the most of them. The clock keeps ticking and life is not for the faint-hearted. So, after hibernating for a couple of winters, I decided to indulge in the Canadian dream of a country cottage. This cottage, however, would be for year-round use, a summer getaway from the city, walks in the woods, visits to a local farm to pick sweetcorn straight off the stalks and five minutes from a scenic golf course. It would also be a ski chalet, close to the ski slopes and the après-ski bonhomie.

It worked and it didn't. Moving in the week before hunting season was not smart. We awoke, not to the sound of birds singing in the trees, but to a replay of Ho Chi Minh's final assault on Saigon. Lunatics with pump-action shotguns and Jim Bowie hunting knives were behind every tree in our woods, cleverly disguised in orange vests, blasting away at anything that moved. Not a single leaf rustling in the breeze was safe.

Fortunately, the hunting season is brief and, after taking my own pot shots at porcupines with an airgun, trying to discourage their appetite for the wooden siding on the cottage, I settled in for a placid interlude. Then the new neighbours arrived.

Their cottage was around a hundred metres away and they were to be permanent residents, commuting to and from work. Perfect, thought I. They will keep an eye on the place during the week and give a quick phone call in the event that lightning strikes or lurking Indians look ready to chop the house down and turn it into a totem pole. Not very PC, I admit.

I invited them in for a getting-to-know-you drink and the man of the cottage turned out to be an armourer, stationed at a nearby Canadian military camp, but living off base. No security worries here. He seemed to dress permanently in camouflage gear, with glossy black army boots you could see your face in, a crew cut and tattoos covering every inch of exposed skin. Nobody was going to mess with the sergeant major.

He did, however, have a rather quaint hobby connected with his work, which I found a bit hard to enthuse about. He was a serious collector of military ammunition, from 18th-century musket balls to modern automatic mercury-tipped rifle bullets and even tank and artillery shells. Fair enough, I supposed. Each to his own. But when he invited us round for a reciprocal cup of tea, he insisted on showing me his prized collection and took me down to the basement, where crates of live ammunition were stored from floor to ceiling and wall to wall. And – ohmigod! – it was all stored in the utility room where an oil-fired furnace blasted heat through forced air pipes throughout the house all winter… We were suddenly spending our weekends next to the next Hiroshima and could be vapourised any minute. Fortunately summer came and the bomb unit was transferred to another posting.

The spring assault of blackflies is a minor distraction. Admittedly, the tiny little pinhead-sized monsters swarm around your head in their thousands the minute you step outside, clogging up your nose and ears and biting remarkably large chunks of skin off your body for such minute creatures, but they only survive for about two weeks before mosquitoes the size of bats arrive and eat them – and then settle in for the rest of the summer, turning their attention to drilling for blood on the human feeding grounds.

Summer turns to fall, the most beautiful time of year, when the leaves change from green to myriad shades of yellow, orange and red. But it is a precursor to Mr Frosty – and I mean *Mr Frosty*. I have to admit, the snow-drenched winter is why I blew the bank account on the chalet. We could ski to our hearts' content and it was just five minutes away. Even better, there was a floodlit ski run, so we could ski at night.

But it didn't start well. My wife, a novice, fell off the chair lift on our first run and then had to be rescued by the ski patrol when she disappeared into a mound of straw bales after veering off course on the very gentle nursery slope. That was it for her; she never put on the skis again.

Never mind. I could do the occasional bit of skiing during the day and make up the enforced time shopping and searching for non-existent Michelin-starred restaurants at night, right?

The rose-tinted ski goggles soon misted up. Nobody told me the floodlit ski run was a mogul run, moguls being those nasty little and not-so-little bumps dotted around the slopes just to make them a bit more exciting. That may be fine during the day but, at night, the snow, which had melted on the surface during the midday sun, turned to ice as hard as concrete and the lights could not create the shadows that allow you to spot the moguls before you hit them. A couple of ruptured discs later and that was the end of the night-time excursions.

Sport is almost as much of a religion in Canada as it is in South Africa but, of course, like everything else, it is different. The national obsession is ice hockey, the point of which seems to be to remove your opponents' teeth with swinging sticks or flying pucks, give them whiplash by coming from behind and driving your horizontal stick into their backs, and crush their ribs by smashing them with ferocious body-checks into the boards surrounding the rink. The language the players use would make a navvy blush and makes notoriously foul-mouthed soccer players look like a bunch of choir boys. Most South Africans would probably not want to take their kids to a hockey game and sit within hearing distance of the skating gladiators.

There are moments of levity, however. I used to watch games from a private box owned by the company I worked for. We would sit, drinks and snacks in hand, behind reinforced mirrored glass to watch the game, and the most interesting action came between periods of play, when the fans would get up and move around to stretch their legs. Invariably, unsuspecting women would wander up to the mirror to patch up their make-up, pick their teeth or readjust contact lenses, to the hilarity and ribald remarks of the uncouth oafs – me included – on the other side of the glass.

Canadian football, similar to American football but with even more obscure rules and regulations, and basketball, a truly stupid pastime – which I delighted in referring to as netball, just to goad its intellectually deprived fans – also have a following. But baseball is the other sport with widespread support, and Canadian teams have had some significant success in the largely American-dominated game.

It's not cricket, but I must confess to a soft spot for the round bat and the subtleties of the contest. The only problem is the fans. They have ants in their pants and simply cannot sit still. Every five minutes they are up on their feet, pushing past to get another gallon container of Coke, a foot-long hotdog and an ice cream or a sackfull of popcorn. They spend more time in search of fast food to fill the void below their belts than watching the game. So I took to watching on television. I missed the atmosphere of actually being there but I didn't miss the frustration of waiting for the other fans to choke on their bloody popcorn.

When you talk about Canada, you cannot get away from the issue of weather. Across the country, spring is very brief, often mixed with wintry conditions; summer is usually fantastic, except for frequent rain on the west coast, but lasts for only about three months; fall – a.k.a. autumn – is a blissful time of year; and then winter sets in for a good seven months.

In the Maritime Provinces and Newfoundland, on the east coast, there is snow, rain and cold. Quebec gets numbingly cold and has lots of snow. Ontario is much the same, although usually not quite as cold – cold, in Canadian terms, being relative. The Prairie Provinces, in central Canada, are as cold as anywhere, except when the warm Chinook wind unexpectedly blows in for a brief respite. British Columbia is not quite so cold, with snow that tends to melt much sooner than other parts of the country, and lots of rain. And if you ever make it to The North – Yukon, Northwest Territories and Nunavut – you will discover what even Canadians consider to be extreme cold.

When I refer to cold as being relative, I think of my first visit to Winnipeg. Early on a February morning, I was waiting, teeth chattering, at the main intersection: Portage and Main, reputedly the coldest city intersection on Earth. As I waited, a man ran out of an office building opposite, unplugged his car's block heater, which had been plugged into an electrical socket in the parking meter, to prevent the engine oil from freezing, and drove away. His car bounced up and down and, turning to a man standing next to me, I observed that the car seemed to have a flat tyre. No it didn't, he responded, it had four flat tyres, but they would get sorted out after he had driven for a while and they'd warmed up. This is a common occurrence in the area and is the result of the car having been parked long enough for the tyres to have developed frozen flat spots where they had borne the weight of the car on the road!

Commuting to and from work poses its own challenges during winter. Not that you get cold. I used to climb into the car in my garage, drive into the underground garage at the office, then take the lift up to my office. At lunchtime, I would take the lift down to a basement level, where there was a virtual underground city with restaurants, shops, banks and any other service you may require. No exposure to the great outdoors at all. Mind you, the sealed office buildings posed their own hazards.

Windows could not be opened to let in any fresh air and the central air-conditioning and heating systems, which continuously pump re-circulated air around the buildings in a similar way that commercial aircraft recycle air, cause viruses that poleaxe employees on a revolving basis. It has created what has become a recognised phenomenon: sick building syndrome.

As long as the roads were clear, getting to the office was relatively painless – I only lived ten minutes away. But getting out of the garage was not always so easy. If it snowed heavily in the night, my contract with a local garage to clear my driveway with a snowplough-equipped Jeep took care of that. The problem came when the huge city snowploughs would then come past, clearing the roads. This involved pushing the snow to the side of the road; that is, into the entrance to my drive. I then would arise to the sight of a one-and-a-half-metre mound of snow blocking the drive. And it would usually have frozen solid by this stage, necessitating an hour of chopping with an axe and digging with a spade before I could get on to the road. It sure didn't lead to a harmonious start to the day.

Politics is always a popular dinner table topic no matter where you live, and Canada is no exception. South Africa is not alone. Canada has its own politicians who are corrupt, self-serving, bumptious and inept, and I have more than a few personal experiences I could relate to illustrate each of those qualities, and at the highest levels. But the most discussed political issue of all is that of Quebec, the French language and the separatist movement.

French Canadians have never forgiven General Wolfe for kicking their French forebears off the Heights of Abraham. But they have an influence at national or federal political level that far exceeds their numbers. While the English language dominates the rest of the country, French is jealously guarded in Quebec, where French-only signage is dictated by law and an English-speaking Canadian will get very short shrift if he does not at least attempt to stumble through his schoolboy French when dealing with shopkeepers or other service providers in the province.

Of course, there is a strong separatist movement in this part of the country. There is, in fact, a separatist political party, which wants to break away from the rest of the country. Although there have been a number of referenda on the subject, Quebeckers have so far voted to remain. But they continue to demand special privileges from the federal government and openly say that whatever they are given will never be enough. Sound familiar?

Native Indians – or, to be PC, First Nations – are another target of popular dissent. They have been awarded huge tracts of land, with enormous mineral resources; they don't pay any taxes; they open casinos close to the borders of their reserves; they illegally sell duty-free cigarettes and liquor; they get large government grants for almost anything they want; and they are drunks who don't work – or so the popular perception goes. Also sound familiar?

So, Canada is really just another failure of the feelgood concept of multiculturalism. Unlike the United States where, despite ethnic and language disputes, an American is an American first and foremost and voluntarily so, Canada disperses into historic groupings. It is like Britain, where large numbers of immigrant groups seek to and are, maybe mistakenly, allowed to establish their mores, languages and customs, and congregate in specific, sometimes ghetto-like areas of major cities. Then when they seek and are granted heritage language education and grants and privileges, which are perceived to impose on and threaten the way of life of the established majority, the problems arise.

To traditional Canadians, those whose ancestors arrived and drew the political boundaries, as opposed to the native Canadians, who were there before that plot of land was called Canada, a Canadian looks and talks and acts like Sergeant Bruce. And that's what the rest of the world thinks they are like, too.

In that sense, it is like Australia. But that is where the likeness and multicultural liberalism ends. In Australia, they enforce the melting pot, except nothing in it melts together. There, they believe that you must look like an Aussie, talk like an Aussie, act like an Aussie and accept the Aussie way or clear off back to where you came from. Canadians are far too polite for that, no matter what they may feel beneath the tolerant public face.

Whether or not anybody who has lived in Canada would go back is an individual choice, based on personal views and experiences. A lot of people would consider going back; it depends on changing circumstances specific to each person. Despite the title of this book, the phrase never say never comes to mind. Today I would not, tomorrow I might.

I know well many of the countries teeming with South African ex-pats. I was born and raised in the UK, lived many years in Canada, travelled extensively and often in the US and have visited Australia many times. And I must declare that South Africa offers things that none of those places do. But, when you gotta go, you gotta go and, despite its foibles, if it ever comes to that, for me, Canada wins hands down.

People may think it is boring when the good guy always wins but, when the chips are down and the Barbarians are at the gate, it's comforting to know the Mounties always get their man.

Canada is the perpetual wallflower that stands on the edge of the hall, waiting for someone to come and ask her for a dance.

– Kevin Myers

In any world menu, Canada must be considered
the vichyssoise of nations, it's cold, half-French, and
difficult to stir.

– *Stuart Keate*

I don't even know what street Canada is on.

– *Al Capone*

WHY I'LL NEVER LIVE IN
OZ AGAIN

BY RICK CROSIER

Rick Crosier's genuine cane toad change purse…

AUTHOR PROFILE

Rick Crosier is a freelance
journalist and filmmaker.
He has been published in
a variety of publications,
including *Men's Health* and
GQ, and is author of *Getting
Away With Murder*. Over the
years, he has lived in Brisbane
and Melbourne, "because he
has family there", and New
Orleans, "because he's a
deviant". He's been back in
South Africa since 2002.

When I was first told we were moving to Australia, I believe my exact words were, "You've got to be bloody kidding!" Why could we not just move somewhere normal, like Afghanistan? I did not want to live in a country whose inhabitants wrestled crocodiles for sport, wore hats with corks attached to strings to ward off flies, and walked around saying "G'day, mate" and "Good on yer". Billy Connolly, a frequent visitor, had recently described the place as "so fucking fraught with danger it's amazing any of them make it to adulthood at all". This is not a comforting testimony. Nor is the fact that Australia produced Rolf Harris.

But to Australia I was destined to go, on and off, for four unforgettable years, as there lived a great portion of the Crosier clan. I quickly discovered that it was a strange place with a vast area called The Bush, which contained, at least as far as I could see, no actual bushes. It had the world-famous Sydney Opera House, but from their reputation for culture it would have been hard enough to round up an orchestra, let alone an audience. No, this was a nation of flat-accented, stubbie-wearing Neanderthals, with kangaroos leaping around their backyards. Of course, like all stereotypes, this is not entirely true. Some of them do wear long pants to funerals.

My family, unfortunately, chose to move to Brisbane, which is, and I say this with all the fondness I can muster, a wretched place. It is Bellville with a different accent. There is still fierce debate amongst religious scholars over whether Brisbane might not be a modern translation of Purgatory, that interminable place between Heaven and Hell. There are, of course, nice places in Australia (I read this in a guidebook once), it's just that my family chose not to live in one of them. We have a knack for this sort of thing.

Our house, though not big, was at least ugly and poorly built. So that was something. The walls were so thin that if you masturbated, the whole household knew about it. If you had actual sex, well, the neighbourhood would be talking about it for weeks. And when in Australia…

The most important thing about Brisbane is probably that it has an airport, so you can leave. Oh, yes, I hear you say, but that's not fair, what about the Gold Coast. Well, yes. We had a company apartment down there – my uncle worked for one of the bigger breweries. (XXXX-Off was the joke at the time.) The Gold Coast was a bit of an eye-opener. Firstly it didn't have a bookstore, not even in its mall. If you wanted to read anything, your best bet would have been the bus timetable. Stores carrying garishly coloured vests and swimming trunks were, however, in great supply. The level of this ignorance of the finer things manifested itself at a local pawnshop, where the proprietor sold me a perfectly good Tag Heuer for $25. "Oh right, the metal one," he'd said, as though I was absolutely daft for not wanting one of plastic digitals capable of doing everything except keeping track of time.

The first trip to the Gold Coast taught me a great deal about the Australian mentality. It was during what they call Schoolies Week: essentially, the Aussie equivalent of the American Spring Break. So a bacchanal. Wet T-shirt contests, a good deal of drinking and sex on tap. Good times. In amongst all this revelry we decided to go to a local nightclub. This was one of my first lessons in the oddities of Australia (of which there are many). The price of drinks in nightclubs – usually Bundy, the local rum, and Coke – is what an oil baron might describe as "excessive". This is one way to discourage public drinking. As a result, everyone gets liquored-up before they go out, and then usually tries to slip a hip flask in with them. It's not uncommon for the male of the Australian species to tape those little sachets of rum to their inner thighs with surgical tape in order to save themselves a couple of dollars. This results in a truly bizarre spectacle: obviously heterosexual males appearing to explore their genitals in public. And I thought this sort of behaviour only happened in bathhouses where men call each other darling.

The next level of bizarreness is that most Aussie nightclubs I visited had a strict dress code. No T-shirts, no sport shoes, no sense. So what we have here is a spectacle of note: a bunch of well-dressed, half-pissed young people fiddling with their intimate regions while propping themselves up on the bar. It's like a meeting of the Young Republicans.

Australia is, in many regards, the new Sweden. It is one of the most over-legislated countries in the world. You will struggle to find a more regulated society, which is hugely ironic in a nation of such characters (though you might argue that it is, as such, hugely necessary). No-one parks illegally: your car will be impounded and hurled into the Tasman Sea before you've even walked into the shop. No-one speeds: Plod will have you in wrist-bracelets then fine you out of house and home before you can say Waltzing Matilda. No-one drinks and drives: this is even worse than speeding, and the police will attach electrodes to the aforementioned intimate regions before you can say, "G'day, offisher".

Now this is both good and bad. It's entirely logical that you should have laws and that you should enforce them, but when you enforce them as collectively and effectively as the Aussie cops do, it tends to start sucking the life out of the place. And it starts manifesting itself with some peculiar side effects. Take drink-driving. It is a universal no-no across the country and, as a result, a strong taxi culture prevails. But this means everyone gets drunk when they go out. The attitude is, well hell, since I'm not driving, I may as well have a skinful. And so the clubs can be rather dangerous. During the Cold War there was a term MAD, which stood for Mutual Assured Destruction and described the atomic Mexican standoff that kept the Americans and the Russians from ever pushing the button. In South Africa, we employ this defence mechanism when we find ourselves in dodgy establishments surrounded by dodgy people – you never know if the other guy is armed, so you tend to stay in your box. In Oz, you know he's unarmed – the law says he has to be – so you can beat the merry hell out of him if you want without fear of increasing the lead content in your body. And so the Aussies, not a nation known for their love of civilised rational debate, do.

Of course, they've now clamped down on public drunkenness: you may not enter a bar intoxicated and you most certainly may not be served an alcoholic beverage if you are under the influence. But, in this instance, the Australian man's love for a wet one overrides his propensity for bowing to the law; he'll pull out every sneaky trick in the book to get himself his next schooner. And for every soak ejected from a drinking establishment, there are twenty dinkum Aussie blokes hammered beyond belief at the pool table or having a go on the Pokie machines…

This, you must remember, is a nation largely descended from convict stock. Lord knows that's how we Crosiers arrived there. Her Majesty had had quite enough of whatever my ancestors were up to and decided the further away we were, the less trouble we could cause. Though there is no hard evidence, the prevailing theory must have been that we would develop a taste for eucalyptus and spend most of our time asleep, like koalas, thereby not being much of a nuisance to anybody.

This did not work. We're still a blight on society. And like us, there are many, many Australians running about the place with a screw or two loose.

Society in Australia is a strange thing. In South Africa we're used to a class structure, largely economically based. In Australia they're having none of it.

We lived next door to a chap who emptied rubbish bins for a living. He was officially – and I kid you not – a "garbologist". Now this fellow had the sort of education that one normally associates with people named Jethro who have no teeth and sleep with their sisters. In a normal society, and Australia is not one, Jethro and I would not have found ourselves seated across a dinner table, let alone living next door. In Australia they would rather you be a serial killer than a classist. "Hell, mate, it's an honest day's work," is the attitude. Stephen Hawking, should he not wish to be exiled from society, would have to have a barbie with one of those lunkheads from the WWE who make their coin being hit in the face by metal chairs, and pretend like they were intellectual equals. Of course, this works in reverse of course: Lunkhead would have to pretend that Stephen Hawking wasn't paralysed and could execute a pile-driver just as deftly as he. Viva egalitarianism!

This attitude is, naturally, extended to romance and sex. One night, when out with a relative's fiancé and his friends at a local pub, a young lady took a fancy to me. She was, and I say this as a gentleman, of questionable attractiveness, even through beer goggles. This did not deter her in her advances one iota. Nor did the fact that I happened to be dating an attractive lady at the time. The best description of her behaviour comes from an old Humphrey Bogart film: she tried to sit on my lap… while I was standing up.

"Go for it, mate," the fiancé said.

His friend concurred: "A root's a root, gets the old fella wet, doesn't it?"

Being a reserved South African at heart, I had to reject their suggestion, though my reply was suitably Australian. "Not with your dick" was, I believe, the line. And this is the thing: you may or may not end up bedding Aussie slappers, but the Australian manner will start rubbing off on you sooner or later.

This is all not to say that Australia does not manufacture some of the world's most beautiful women. They have after all given us Nicole Kidman, Naomi Watts, Kylie Minogue and Nicole Kidman. Not that I'm stalking her or anything. The attractive lady I was dating at the time would, in my opinion, have given any one of them a run for their money in the looks department. What I *am* saying, though, is that South Africa has a far more plentiful stockpile of beautiful young things. Back in the day, my co-ed high school in Cape Town was like an adolescent Playboy Mansion. In the area in which I now live, the Atlantic Seaboard, beauty is in greater supply than demand. I know women so eye-achingly beautiful that you need to wear dark glasses just to shield yourself from their luminosity – and they can't get modelling jobs. So our conversation is often limited to, "Yes, I'll have another refill, thanks."

This is a key difference between South Africa and Australia, similar to the difference between New York and LA – in Australia there is a premium placed on personality; in South Africa, on looks. This means that, though beautiful women are in shorter supply in Oz, your chances of scoring them are infinitely better. In this regard, I kind of like the egalitarianism that Australia provides.

In Cape Town, you may have heard the commonly quoted statistic that there are seven women to every (straight) man, but has this ever really affected *your* hit rate? South African women are very status oriented. When I tell them I'm a photographer (not actually a lie), well golly, do the eyes light up. Tell them you're a writer, on the other hand, and boy have you just disappeared into the woodwork. You may just as well have told them you were a garbologist. In Australia I never had to make any of my usual shameless plays; the women there really don't care.

Australians have a healthy respect for their artists. I was lucky enough to meet and spend time with the singer Nick Cave, he of the Bad Seeds, and I was one of many who watched Michael Hutchence's funeral. I don't think I have seen a more open display of emotion than when Nick sang *Into My Arms*. Until recently, that is, when this display of genuine feeling was seen on an even greater scale with the passing of Steve Irwin, the Crocodile Hunter. He was, in every sense, the epitome of old-school Australia. A masculine, badly dressed family man who did silly things like mucking around with crocodiles and antagonising deadly snakes ("Don't do this at home!"). His death was not so much one of an individual as it was that of an ideal. Shops closed. Grown men wept openly in the streets. His daughter Bindi gave a speech at his funeral that made the grown men in the streets stop weeping and start blubbing. It was a scene that would have brought a tear to a glass eye. If there is one national trait that I would ascribe to the Australians, it's authenticity of emotion.

Australians like their men to be men and their women to be, well, women. This lack of dissolve between the identity of the sexes strikes me as being inherently healthy. There is no fudging of terms; everyone knows where they stand. If you're behaving like a dunderhead, you'll be informed of as much. In no uncertain terms. If they care for you, they'll let you know. Perhaps not as physically as the Italians, but you still know where you stand in their hearts.

Let's take, as an example, the pre-eminent Australian actor of our time, Russell Crowe. He is the very picture of unapologetic masculinity. However, it is Advanced Masculinity. While actors like Clint Eastwood and Charles Bronson epitomised a masculinity that eschewed emotion, Mr Crowe has taken things a step further. Yes, he has a ranch and rides horses, but this is in reality, not just on screen. Crowe's speech at Steve Irwin's funeral was almost as moving as his daughter's. This is one of the contradictions in Australian society: as a man, you're meant to suck it up and be a man, not a sissy, but when it comes down to the line, well, mate, it's all right to cry.

I cannot imagine anyone, short of Nelson Mandela, whose passing could inspire such an outpouring of grief in South Africa. Steve Hofmeyer? Um, no. Nolene? A crocodile couldn't muster the tears. Not even Johnny Clegg, bless his ear kicks.

The more "masculine" Australians seem to have a serious issue with their sexuality. Footie, rugger, cricket, drinking, all things they do with their mates, which is in itself a rather dodgy term when referring to same-sex interaction. Sure, Frank Sinatra and the rest of the Rat Pack called each other "Baby", as in "You're money, baby," but they didn't spend their Saturday afternoons patting each other on the bottom as a sign of affirmation, and then heading off to shower together. Given this proclivity, it is hardly surprising that Sydney hosts the world's largest gay-pride parade. Cape Town and San Francisco are sloppy seconds in this regard.

In all seriousness, though, your average hetero Aussie male is as straight down the line as you can imagine. For one, he prides himself on his ability to do a good barbie, Oz for braai.

Well, not so much.

It is not, I'm afraid, any substitute for an egte South African braai. Firstly, they favour gas over good old-fashioned wood or charcoal. Then there is the issue of the quality of food. And believe me, it is an issue. The prawns are great. The fish can go either way. And I'm afraid, as far as sausage goes, if you've ever had boerewors – the proper stuff – nothing else will ever compare. Australian sausage is every bit as bad as American. But then what the Americans lack in quality, they certainly make up for in size.

Which brings us to another problem with Australia. Xenophobia. While the Crosier stronghold might have had Stephen Hawking living on the one side, and Lunkhead the WWE wrestler on the other, in reality we tended to associate with Koos van Tonder and Daisy Smit, much the same way the Changs tended to be friends with the Wongs. This, not without reason, irritates the Australians, who feel that if you're going to live in one of the greatest melting pots in the world, you should bloody well do a bit of melting. This has led to the uprising of a lunatic right wing-fringe, whose most notable proponent was a one-time fish-'n'-chips shop owner called Pauline Hanson. Fortunately, she was sent to prison for electoral fraud – well at least until the UN stepped in and decided that her ranting was cruel and unusual punishment for the other prisoners, some of whom may only have been murderers.

See how cleverly we've segued into the issue of crime? Here Oz beats us hands down. Which, admittedly, is not hard. I know only one person in Australia who carries a gun. And he carries it round his vineyard to shoot naughty birds that are trying to attack his grapes. In the process he usually manages to do far more damage to the vines than all the birds in *The Birds* could have managed.

"Bastards! Why can't they just sit still while I shoot them? That just cost me another three bloody bottles of Chardonnay!" he is often heard to bellow. And then he has a fine time searching the many pockets of his hunting vest for more cartridges so he can charge about his vineyard destroying even more Chardonnay.

I suppose everyone must have a hobby.

In Australia, for those who don't spent their leisure time rubbing cricket balls against their own, drugs are really quite popular. Unlike Cape Town, where everyone works in the restaurant, film, modelling or PR industries, and the drug of choice is cocaine, they prefer heroin. This is why they have, in the main, economic-sustenance rather than profit-motivated crimes. Of course, there are biker gangs who get a little enthusiastic in their physical interactions with buyers who skip out on their bills, but mainly it is a country of barroom or maintenance crime.

They do not have, for example, the sort of criminals who invite you, at gunpoint, to step out of your car in order that it might be redistributed to the historically less fortunate. And, as such, they do not have to worry about the type of cars they should buy their daughters based on the basis of hijacking statistics. (My daughter, for example, is going to drive, not the stylish convertible she wants, but rather the dullest Volvo I can find, painted in the most garish colour my local hardware store has to offer. If it's not garish enough, we'll mix another one up. She'll hate me until she's 50, but then she probably would have anyway. So that's fine.)

What you do have to worry about in Oz is coming home to find your daughter with a needle in her arm. The Australians have taken, depending on your stand, either a highly enlightened approach or one that smacks of absolute idiocy: they have established heroin-shooting rooms in clinics and hospitals. Never having taken heroin, I don't pretend to know the ins and outs of it, but it does take a brave government to say, "Here, go get high on the taxpayer's dollar." The wisdom of government-sponsored drugs is one worth pondering. Do I appreciate the presence of disposable-needle dispensaries that dot my neighbourhood? No, I actually find them rather creepy. Do I want to pay an extra tax so that my daughter can get free heroin at a state clinic? Well, actually, I probably do. This way she is in a safe, controlled medical environment, she doesn't have to sell her body on the streets to afford the next fix, and she's not going to be found dead and bloated in some toilet the next morning. She has access to counselling, to emotional and physical help and support. In this respect, Australia is streets ahead of most civilised nations.

But onto sunnier things. What the Good Lord was smoking the day he created Aussie wildlife is his own private mystery. Sure, He was on form when he gave us the giraffe and wildebeest, but when it came to Oz, boy, was He on form. The kangaroo? The wombat? The koala? The duck-billed platypus? And those are just the famous ones. There's also the bearded dragon, the Tasmanian devil, the echidna… These aren't animals; they're extras in a *Star Wars* film.

My aunt, who is a Crosier, and therefore not in the Top Ten when it comes to the mental health stakes, has had most of these creatures at one time or another. To knock on the door only to be greeted by a particularly enthusiastic roo is a rather surreal experience. Almost as bad as finding a sign in the garden reading: *Beware! Here Be Dragons!* And they're not kidding. The dragons in question are those shirty lizards with jaws that puff out into big beards, which scuttle about the Aussie bush like velociraptors. You've seen them on TV. When I saw them for real, I remember thinking, oh my God, I'm in *Jurassic Park*.

One night, I was sleeping in the guest room when I heard a knocking at the door. Strange. I opened the door expecting something normal, you know, like the kangaroo. Turns out it was the wombat. If you've never seen a wombat before, it is one of the cutest creatures on the planet – until it turns into a teenager, when it becomes sulky, antagonistic and stubborn. Like teenagers, then… Wombat and I had not been getting on like a house on fire, so I wasn't too keen on a midnight chat over milk and cookies. I shut the door. But Wombat was having none of this. It simply clawed its way through the door.

What sort of country was I living in?

When I tried to explain the damage to my aunt in the morning, she simply shrugged and said, "Oh, they do that all the time. They're quite willful."

"I'm going to play with the dragons," I said, "Come, kangaroo."

After a nocturnal wombat invasion a man's constitution is not what it ought be. He needs a bit of respite, a bit of relaxing normality. So I jetted off to Lady Elliot Island on the Great Barrier Reef in a plane that did not inspire much confidence. It had graffiti on the inside walls: "Bruce was here". Well, no arguments about that then. With that in mind, the captain's exclamation of "Oh bugger!" did not inspire much comfort as we came in to land on a runway that looked too short by half a mile. And he followed it up, once we'd landed and started breathing again, with a warning to look out for the "stingers and stonies".

What, I wondered, were stingers and stonies?

Lady Elliot Island is one of the most beautiful, tranquil, peaceful places on earth. From end to end it extends probably about four kilometres. It is a nature preservation site. But I'm afraid that I'm not so sure that all nature should be preserved. Flies, mosquitoes, Parktown prawns, politicians – I'm sure we'd all be happier without them. And you can add stingers and stonies to the list.

The stinger, for your edification, is a tiny jellyfish, also known as an irukandji, that stings the hell out of you. This is not hopping-on-one-foot-I've-just-stubbed-my-toe stuff; it's please-just-cut-my-leg-off-already stuff. Not the sort of thing you want to experience when you've just escaped a wombat. Like most venomous Australian creatures, its poison can be fatal, and this little bugger (along with its more famous cousin, the box jellyfish) is, in fact, responsible for keeping swimmers off north Australian beaches during summer. For half the year, in heat that defines the word sweltering, you have to stick to the specially made stinger nets if you want to step into the ocean and have healthy odds of coming back out – not any way to take a dip at the beach, if you ask me.

The stonies – stonefish – are altogether more worrisome. They, as you might imagine, look like stones and, generally speaking, should you step on one, it'll sprout spikes, inject you with poison and your loved ones will have to be informed of your untimely passing. I have never seen a group of paunchy middle-aged people in baggy shorts and inappropriate bikinis inspired to such a display of action as when our guide noticed we had a stonie in our midst. It is possible that our mass stampede from the shallows caused a tidal wave somewhere on the far side of the world.

Oh how I longed for the wombat and the dragons!

Surely, I thought, there must be somewhere on this continent that isn't fraught with immediate physical danger?

Perth.

Perth certainly exists, though to what purpose no-one is really sure. It is, reportedly, the most remote city in the world. I can understand why. It's like one of those people you meet at a dinner party, and then the next day when someone asks you if you remember Trevor, you scratch your head and go, "Trevor? Trevor was *there*?" It makes the sort of impression that butter would make on a diamond.

A lot of South Africans have emigrated to Perth, the old saying being "packing for Perth", when things were not looking so stable in the old country. This is no great testimony to Perth: you must remember that my family, the world being their proverbial oyster, ended up in Brisbane and Tasmania. The only reason I can see for moving to Perth is a perverse attraction for Cape Town's infamous southeaster, the Cape Doctor, an evil, spiteful wind whose twin lives in Perth and goes by the title of Fremantle Doctor. But I'm being mean. Perth is nice, I suppose.

What about Sydney, then? Like Jo'burg, it's rather fast-paced. Or, as I put it, exhausting. But you have to give credit where it's due: Sydney is a top-class city and an international hub for good reason.

It's classy, trendy, the food's great, the vibe's good, and some of it is strikingly beautiful. That said, there are parts of Sydney – affluent areas, too – that come straight out of the Big Book Of Architectural No-Nos. Catch the ferry to Manly from the bustling, impressive Circular Quay, flanked on either side by the imposing Harbour Bridge and the iconic Opera House, and you soon chug past the monstrous apartment blocks of Darling Point and then Rose Bay, an otherwise fancy little Saffer enclave. Sydney also has its Capetonian characteristics, the least attractive of which is the snotty attitude the locals have been known to show to out-of-towners. There's something about popular, model-dense cities that seems to suggest to their inhabitants they should be scornful of those not privileged enough to reside among them. Very unAustralian – which, you'll be charmed to know is an actual word. Seriously. As in "Dropping your litter in the street is unAustralian, mate." Honestly, what other country could get away with that?

Ah, the idiosyncrasies of the Aussies. It's their one real strong point. We expect them to be mad. I personally own an Australian bearded dragon, Tara, as well as a change purse made out of a cane toad. That is, the toad had its hindquarters removed, a zipper was added, and that's the purse. These possessions, I have been told by independent auditors, are "not normal". To someone of Australian origin, however, they are the very picture of normality. And I've only lived there for a few years! If this book sells well enough, expect a kangaroo to open when you knock on my door.

So Sydney is very different from Brisbane. Your dinner has names rather than numbers. Your literacy skills are deemed good enough not to have to point at pictures when the waitress comes round to take your order.

Which brings us to what is probably called "the nutritionally designated arm of the hospitality profession" or some such rot. In Australia being a waiter is a profession, not just something to keep you in beer money. I forget who wrote that wonderful line about the surly waiter with his eye on the clock and his thumb in your soup, but in Australia, that just doesn't happen. If the world ever has a shortage of such commodities, there'll be an exportable stockpile of note.

This, of course, defies any logical explanation. In Oz, waiters are salaried; they don't rely on tips for their living, there isn't anything on your bill reading Gratuity Not Included. Even if the service is superb, they do not expect a tip. It is what it really should be, a show of gratitude for exceptional service. The last time I was there, I tried to tip a particularly exceptional waitress. She looked embarrassed, as though I were some crass American or German tourist who liked to throw small change at the feet of the Natives. Go on, gather up the pennies. By offering to give her a gratuity I had rather insulted her.

"Actually, sir, we don't work that way here."

She had performed the task she was charged with, and for which she was paid, and here I was treating her like a charity case. It was demeaning for her. I apologised and explained that in South Africa, waiters expected a tip as par for the course.

"But don't they get paid?" she asked.

Well, actually, no. Our waiters are dependent on the benevolence of those to whom they bring dinner and drinks. In other words, theirs is performance-related income. It is a leisure/entertainment industry, and I still cannot understand the difference in attitudes between Australia and South Africa. Logically, if your monthly take-home is guaranteed by not getting the wrong plate to the wrong table too often, what's your worry? Do the bloody minimum and cash the paycheck. If it's dependent on the goodwill of your customers, you'll bend over backwards to ensure their charity, which is really what a tip is.

In Australia they don't understand this concept. An Aussie friend of mine put it in less delicate terms: "You South Africans are mad. You pay people to bring you food that you've already overpaid for? For God's sake, I'd just walk into the kitchen and pick it up myself. And then you tip some guy who manages to pour most of your beer into vaguely the right glass without spilling too much of it? The legacy of apartheid is the least of your problems, mate."

Possibly. But funny you mention that, because you guys have some political problems of your own.

U2 had a line in one of their songs, before they stopped making good records: "We look to the past when the future dries up." Australians are facing just this problem with their guilt-laden, politically correct approach to the "Aboriginal problem". Like the New Zealand Maoris, the Abbos (as they shouldn't really be called any more), are making claims to vast tracts of Australian land. They were there first, you see.

In South Africa we have this idea of "the level playing field." In America, it's "everyone is born equal". Both of these are, on the evidence, rubbish. We are not born equal: ask Helen Keller. Or Tiger Woods. Now, sure you can argue that Mr Mugabe is right and what's yours is really mine, but this is the sort of dialogue my boxer dogs have. The one has the tennis ball, the other one wants it. So he barks incessantly until, out of sheer frustration or just the desire for a bit of peace and quiet, the first one gives it to him.

I suppose, it's just the way of the world these days; something to get used to and deal with. And it wouldn't be such a problem if Australia hadn't jumped in the PC boat and hoisted such a huge sail. Now in order to qualify for any number of taxpayer-sponsored freebies, all you have to do is prove you're one sixteenth Aboriginal. Gosh, I think my great-grandfather once shook hands with an Aboriginal, can I have some money?

The answer, probably: yes.

In a country that has so much open space just waiting to be given away, and inhabited by such sensible (if idiosyncratic) people, you'd think they could breeze over this issue of reparations, especially when you realise just how few Aboriginals there are: two per cent of the population. And yet it is a permanent sticking point. The Australian taxpayer resents sponsoring the housing and education of people who, the common perception has it, make little or no contribution to society, and are mostly drunks, to boot. This is the prevailing attitude.

From my point of view, I am aware that the Aboriginal culture has given the world a couple of unique items, mainly the boomerang and the didgeridoo. The boomerang – and like any good Australian, I own many – is one of the most bizarre inventions on the planet. It is designed, at least in my experience, to hit its user on the head. So God help you if you're not wearing a motorcycle helmet.

The didgeridoo. Oh dear. I love music, but this, like the djembe drum, is not music. I would rather listen to my three-year-old nephew banging pots and pans together in the kitchen than a didge session. It really is the most irritating infernal racket, and here I'm including Eminem.

But that's neither here nor there. The point is, a century or so after they weren't even included on the national census (sheep were!), the Abbos remain "a problem". In the context of South Africa's tumultuous recent past, and the fact that we have eleven different languages and all sorts of complex racial rivalry going on, our ex-pats struggle to cope with this relatively simple issue. It really is too much, because it's too much about too little.

Fortunately, the great Aboriginal debate is confined, mostly, to the Northern Territories, to Darwin and thereabouts. And along with Adelaide and Hobart, Darwin doesn't really count.

So we come to Melbourne which, in addition to being the jewel in Australia's crown, is also Little Europe. Melbourne is as civilised as Australia gets. My girlfriend at the time lived in St Kilda, which is like Toulouse, a haven of good restaurants, friendly people, art and students. There was also a rather interesting S&M club, Hellfire, where, bizarrely, we met a famous American actor whose name rhymes with George Clooney. Different strokes for different folks, if you'll excuse the pun. I am enjoined from mentioning what he, my girlfriend and I got up to, but then you probably read about it in some tabloid or other. I'm the one with the mask on his face.

I've been rather harsh on Australia, but it's the harshness of one brother criticising the other. Deep down we love each other; our criticism comes out of a heartfelt affection. This is something Australians understand. Shake your head and call someone you know a "useless fucking monkey", and they know you care for them. Say, "I love you mate", and they know you're drunk.

Take their national anthem. It is, apparently, called *Advance Australia Fair*. I don't know if I've ever even heard it. Certainly I know that Aussies at sporting events where its played look a bit bewildered. Bring on *Waltzing Matilda*, however, and you'll have a choir to make the Welsh quiver in their boots.

But the key question, the title of this book remains unanswered: why, indeed, will I never live in Oz again? I honestly don't know. On paper it all seems hunky-dory.

Except that my daughter will become a heroin addict, my wife will be arrested for drink-driving after her second sherry and my taxes will be spent on the production of boomerangs and didgeridoos for the benefit of hopeless Aboriginals who are living on land I have no claim to. Whereafter I will doubtless become addicted to gambling, as 99 per cent of the Australian population happens to be. Which means I will have to spend inordinate amounts of time on the Pokie machines or sports betting and, of course, investing in adult diapers… To make matters worse, I will have to be nice to people. I do not like being nice to people. In Australia you have to.

If I want to buy my Sunday paper, I want to buy it, go home, sit on the couch and read it. I do not particularly care about the vendor's family history or how her day's been. I do not fancy a chat with the till-jockey when I'm buying loo paper.

In fact, I must conclude, the only real reason for living in Australia is having been sent there at Her Majesty's Pleasure. And then being too lazy to leave.

The Australian Book Of Etiquette is a very slim volume.

– Paul Theroux

I'd like to be seen as an average Australian bloke… I can't think of a nobler description of anybody than to be called an average Australian bloke.

– *John Howard*

God bless America. God save the Queen. God defend New Zealand. And thank Christ for Australia.

– *Russell Crowe*

WHY I'LL NEVER LIVE IN
NEW ZEALAND
AGAIN

BY TIM RICHMAN

Auckland skyline snapshot, taken from Mission Bay

AUTHOR PROFILE

Tim Richman is a journalist
and managing editor of the
Two Dogs book imprint.
He has written for a variety
of local and international
publications, and is co-author
of *Don't Climb Kilimanjaro…
Climb The Ruwenzori.* He has
lived in Auckland, Sydney
and Vancouver, "all worthy
experiences", though for him
"Cape Town will always
be home".

Friends of mine, Pierre and Wendy, visited New Zealand for a month while on their extended honeymoon in 2005. They arrived in March, from South America, headed south from Auckland, and spent most of their time exploring the immensely beautiful South Island in a camper van. They cycled among the wine estates of Marlborough, went jet-boating in Shotover Canyon, sea-kayaked along the spectacular Abel Tasman coastline, saw the incomparable Milford Sound, fished, hiked and generally had a whale of a time.

When I met up with Pierre and Wendy in Sydney, where I was living at the time, they described their stay as one of the most memorable in all their travels. And they've done a lot of travelling: all over central and southern Africa, most of the European centres, a stint in southeast Asia, six months in South America; you name it, they've done it. Sitting down over whiskies in the Town Hall Hotel pub in Balmain, they only had superlatives for New Zealand: beautiful countryside, great food, fantastic wine, friendly people, so much to do, amazing weather…

My maternal family hails from New Zealand, and having visited that part of the world probably ten or twelve times since the early eighties, including living and working in Auckland in 2000/2001, I know the country well. So I can vouch for a lot of what Pierre and Wendy were saying. It *does* have its amazing qualities and attractions, and I can well recommend it as a holiday destination, particularly a few weeks trundling about the South Island. But perhaps the whisky had distorted my senses, because I had never heard anyone talk so enthusiastically about New Zealand before. It wasn't right; enthusiasm and New Zealand are incongruous. I was missing something here.

Hang on, what was that about amazing weather?

It turns out that, in a little over a month, Pierre and Wendy had been rained on a mere three times. The rest of the time, they had enjoyed balmy late-summer weather: glorious sunshine and hardly a breath of wind to disturb their peregrinations. I was astounded. Could this be the same country where I had spent two of the past twenty-five years of my life? Where were the days of persistent drizzle, the squalls, the battering winds?

Whenever I mention Pierre and Wendy's trip to my brother, he is even more dumbfounded than me. Aggrieved, actually. Like me, he has never experienced an extended period of fine New Zealand weather. In December of 2000, for example, he and his girlfriend arrived in the country and spent some time at the family beach house outside Wanganui, on the southwest coast of the North Island, before also heading south. In a little over six weeks, they did not go two consecutive days without rain. It was so bad that they made a point of keeping count. And that was the middle of summer… But here were Pierre and Wendy, Kiwi virgins, arriving to the most glorious month of New Zealand sunshine in recorded history – then having the cheek to describe the country's weather as "amazing".

For the record, it is not. My charmed newly wed friends had, in fact, had the good fortune of arriving at the back end of one of the country's worst summers in recent history, showing up just in time for the first few weeks of fine weather in over a year. Another friend of mine had made the trip out to New Zealand the December before to climb Mount Cook, its highest peak, and didn't get the chance; the storms were too severe. Suffice it to say, his experience is a lot more in keeping with the traditional Kiwi climate.

Complaining about the inadequacies of another country's weather seems to be one of the greatest clichés of the pro-South African argument. But, by their nature, there is truth in cliché. And New Zealand's weather is particularly apt because it literally dictates the Kiwi lifestyle, even its conversation. It is, I reckon, an appropriate metaphor for the country as a whole. So bear with me a moment longer.

I am frequently amazed by the perception that many South Africans hold of life in New Zealand. Before spending a summer in Vancouver, I'd expected a pleasant stay among friendly enough people in an interesting city. Admittedly, the word "nice" had figured in my thoughts. And I wasn't too far off the mark. If anything, it was nicer than I'd expected. Point is, I suspect most visitors to Canada know what they're in for, more or less. So how come so many Saffers seem to have the wrong impression of New Zealand? They envision a smaller, greener island version of South Africa, with Maoris instead of black people and sheep instead of wildlife. And where they sound like Australians. Similar weather to SA, though perhaps not quite as warm; similar outdoor lifestyle, similar outlook on life. Well, make the man some bloody eggs, because you're wrong, wrong and wrong.

First of all, let's get the accents out of the way. Spend some time with Australians and New Zealanders and you'll soon realise how very different they sound. If you're ever in doubt, there's a sure-fire test to tell them apart: Australians say "feesh 'n' cheeps", New Zealanders "fsh 'n' chps". The similarity is in their mutual inflection at the end of sentences – like they're asking a question? Otherwise, regular Aussie and Kiwi accents are as different as league and union. In fact, Kiwis love having a go at the Aussies about the way they talk; it's part of the mutual respect-antagonism that the two countries have for each other, and which has manifested itself in an inferiority complex of sorts, particularly for many Aucklanders who wished they were as fancy as the Sydneysiders or Melbournites. It's a theme that constantly resurfaces. But for now, back to the weather.

Invariably – unless you're Pierre and Wendy – rain welcomes you to New Zealand. You survive the three-and-a-half-hour flight from Sydney easily enough (or the ten-hour haul from Kuala Lumpur with a little more difficulty), and drop down through the swirling grey mist and cloud to green fields, and when you make your way out of Auckland International Airport, it's raining. But it's not proper rain, like a Highveld thunderstorm or a savage Cape cold front that belts down with all the sound and fury of real commitment. No: this is a fine drizzle that drifts as much as it falls; peters out, then resumes on a whim. If you look up to the heavens, you might notice patches of blue-skied potential and the threat of fine weather ahead, and you don't even need to break stride on the way to the taxi rank because it's hardly enough to wet your hair.

If you're lucky enough to arrive in a clear spell, chances are the rain will be falling by the time the Sky Tower comes into view on your way into the city. Little wonder that Aucklanders carry their fold-up umbrellas wherever they go, even when the sun is shining, and that Neil and Tim Fynn wrote the Crowded House classic *Four Seasons In One Day* about their home town:

Four seasons in one day;
Lying in the depths of your imagination,
Worlds above and worlds below,
The sun shines on the black clouds hanging over the Domain;
Even when you're feeling warm,
The temperature could drop away,
Like four seasons in one day.

Oh yes indeed.

So you walk a while longer – 15 minutes through the tree-lined Domain, say, or up the Parnell Road hill, from the bridge to Pandoro bakery (where they make the best chocolate brownie known to mankind), or a year along the parks and pavements of Auckland – and it starts to tell. The wetness collects in the creases and folds of your jacket, under your chin and down your neck – weighing you down, weighing you down – and one day you realise it has seeped into your soul and there's nothing the brief patches of sun can do to alleviate it. If you think about it for a moment, it's as though someone somewhere isn't doing his job properly… That about sums up the place.

But before I explain myself, let me take a moment to focus on the little things. Sometimes the details really do count.

Since the 1990 publication of Rian Malan's anguished ode to South Africa, *My Traitor's Heart* (Vintage), the book has entered the realm of "essential reading" for anyone looking for some meaningful understanding of the country in its historical and political context. Malan grapples with the paradoxical love and repugnance he feels for South Africa, explaining how his conscience led him into self-imposed exile in 1977, and how he was compelled to return in the mid-eighties due to an undeniable longing for his homeland. "In America, my soul was desiccated," he writes, describing how he felt before his return. Of course, the political context of the time, as well as the author's extended family's involvement in South Africa's turbulent history – he is related to DF Malan, among others – underscores much of his writing.

In mid-2001, when I read the book for the first time, having been out of the country for a year, I was less interested in Malan's moral quandary than understanding why he longed for home. And it was the little things that grabbed my imagination:

And so I found myself yearning for South Africa. I yearned for the reckless jol, for rutted dirt roads and lonely farmhouses; for the clank of a windmill, the sound of Afrikaans, clouds towering over the Karroo; for the peculiar quality of African light, harsh and piercing; for the smell and look of Johannesburg after rain; and for my Uncle Ben's farm, the memory of which twisted in my heart like a knife, for its loneliness and foreboding, and the blackened plain on which it stood. I longed for Wicks bubble gum, radio serials, Mrs H S Ball's homemade chutney, biltong, Lion beer, a pipe of Durban poison...

Sitting on the Link bus on the way home from the language school where I taught English to Japanese, Chinese, Korean and Swiss students, I too would consider what I missed most about South Africa. The little things that it made it all worthwhile.

As a Capetonian, Table Mountain was the obvious one, in all its guises: lit up at night in summer; brooding in grey cloud in winter; seen from the distance, on a fine day, against the clear blue Cape sky – "1983 Ford Cortina blue", as my friend John describes it. Whatever the façade, there is magic in that mountain.

Then there are the beaches, another obvious call. Clifton Second, with Lion's Head standing guard above, throwing off its colourful hang-gliders and paragliders. Conversely, there's the walk up Lion's Head and the view down to Clifton – or to Robben Island or to the Hottentot Hollands. A half-hour hike, and the city is in the palm of your hands. Cape Town: the stinking heat of the City Bowl on a hot day in summer; the thunder of drumming rain in winter. The oak trees in Newlands Avenue. The buck grazing on the slopes of Groote Schuur as the cars flow below – then looking for newly docked ships as the harbour comes into view around Hospital Bend. The penguins at Boulders, the road to Betty's Bay...

And beyond that, South Africa. Yes, there's biltong. And boerewors and braais. And Coca-Cola – because it does taste different here. And swimming pools. And SuperSport: hands down, the best sports channel in the world. And lunch at Giovanni's among the models and shady Europeans. And talking shit with mates on a Sunday after cricket at Kelvin Grove. And the fucking great, big wild of Africa, with its lions and elephants and crocodiles and baobabs and acacias and bushveld, buzzing and humming and spreading north for a thousand miles.

To be fair, I must compare the little treasures of New Zealand; after all, that is what we're doing here. So what do I miss from the other side of the world, a day-and-a-half's travel away? Pavlova. Ever since eating seven helpings of my grandmother Lorraine's pavlova at Christmas 1986 in Wellington, it haunts my dreams. To the point that the last time I visited for Christmas, in 2005, I got her to rustle up another one. She was eighty-four at the time, so she got her minder, a lawn-mowing, leaf-blowing freak of energy called Betty to do it. But I still considered it Lorraine's pavlova. Plus there's Hokey Pokey ice cream, Kiribati cheeses and just about every Kiwi dairy product every made. Later, affinities for New Zealand beer (Mac's Gold), white wine (Cloudy Bay Sauvignon Blanc) and sushi were discovered, as well as those Pandoro brownies at the top of Parnell Hill. And the organic food in general is incredible. (Saffers have been stupidly slow on the uptake in this department; we don't know what we're missing.)

Anything not food-related? Tricky... Frequent *Simpsons* reruns, considerate drivers, clean streets, green fields (and I mean *green* fields), fantails, sheep (they give you a sense of sleepy contentment), going to the races with my grandfather.

Of course, there's the fantastic running rugby, at all levels. Plus rugby commentary and reporting that puts our hacks to shame. On that note, I should add that rugby fanaticism in New Zealand is as virulent as in South Africa, if not more so; *everyone* is a fan. Scratch the idea of a braai where the guys watch the game while the girls sit around gossiping and drinking white wine with ice. There, it's a barbecue, for starters, and the girls drink beer, watch the game and cheer as loud as anyone. My grandfather JA, who is eighty-five, still gets up in the middle of the night to watch All Black-Springbok test matches. And a loss, rare as it is these days, is enough to truly crush the spirit of the country. The Springbok victory over the All Blacks in the 1995 World Cup final was enough to send countless New Zealanders to therapy. I know; I was there. (A huge regret, but it was, at least, the second-best country in the world to be in.) This is because Kiwis only have two activities that raise genuine passion in their bones: rugby and America's Cup yachting.

But enough with the positives of New Zealand living. Because there were a host of little negatives that ran through my mind on those Link bus journeys; the minor irritants that accumulate over time, weighing you down and crushing your soul.

The longest ad breaks imaginable. Though Sky TV, New Zealand's DSTV equivalent, is more bearable, the free-to-air stations have no trace of shame. Television commercial breaks are insanely long; often long enough to take a shower without missing anything, as I've done on occasion. The eight o'clock Saturday night feature movie on TV3, for example, generally has thirty to thirty-five minutes of commercials, while there is – deviously – no break between the end of one prime-time show and the start of the next so that, when they do come, the actual breaks can last longer. Until you've watched a few months of New Zealand television, you cannot comprehend how frikking annoying this is.

Leaf blowers. Contender for worst invention of all time, the leaf blower seems to me to be the perfect illustration of the depths to which the bored modern man has sunk in order to entertain himself. It is a truly retarded device, and at nine o'clock on a Sunday morning the DIY-loving Kiwi man and his leaf blower generates aggravation on a nuclear scale.

The beaches. Auckland beaches are, in virtually every aspect, the opposite of the Cape's. I headed out to Mission Bay a couple of times for some sun, sea and sand. At the time, it was rated the third-best beach in Auckland, one and two being about an hour's drive away. Though I appreciated that it was quite clean, I cannot think of a worse beach that I've been to. Ever. And this is not hyperbole.

Now consider the nine-minute burn time. After days of persistent drizzle or gusting wind, the sun comes out, the temperature cranks up to a headline-grabbing 26 degrees and you decide to make the effort to actually go to one of the vaguely bearable beaches around Auckland. There aren't many of them, so it's crowded when you get there, but man, you're desperate for some time by the sea, and you're going to spend your afternoon on this three-metre wide steep-angled bank of coarse, grubby sand if it kills you. And it might well just do that, because the New Zealand sun is as harsh as it gets. The ozone being thinner the further south you go, there is very little natural atmospheric protection from the sun when you take off your top in New Zealand. There is no warming sensation of sun on skin; it actually prickles. Even a stroll to the shops without a hat and sun cream can be dangerous. And so weather reports usually conclude with the following day's estimated burn times: the time it will take before your skin starts burning if you don't have protection. The worst I recall seeing was nine minutes, though I seldom watched the reports, as they depressed me – and you generally knew Auckland's forecast anyway: scattered showers, humid, high of 22 degrees...

Note how I've got on to the weather again. As I've mentioned, it really is a Kiwi conversation point. So, on a related note, let me mention New Zealand women.

Another South African misconception is that Kiwi girls are as ugly as sin. This is not entirely true. I've met many pretty Kiwi girls in my time; it's just that they make no effort. The weather is bad for fifty weeks of the year, which means they stay covered up in woollen jumpers and jeans most of the time. And when it does clear up for a day, there's hardly a beach or swimming pool to sit next to. So what's the point of going to gym and staying in shape? Even putting on make-up and going to the hairdresser seems too much to ask.

The knock-on effect is amazing: Kiwi blokes are sadder for it. They have very little to keep them on their toes, to give them a spark and brighten up their day; and so they, too, make less effort – checked shirt, jeans, hiking boots is standard attire. When I say I missed the beaches of Cape Town, I missed the lookers in bikinis as much as anything.

Hmm, suddenly these reasons aren't looking so minor any more. In fact, I'm already scratching at the heart of what I consider to be the fundamental Kiwi flaw. Let me get to it, then.

If you've never visited Auckland, The City Of Sails, a city of close on a million-and-a-half souls, its most striking feature is undoubtedly the Auckland Sky Tower, a tall and gracious edifice that reaches into the sky towards the Long White Cloud above it. It literally leaves all the other buildings around it in its shadow; there seems barely a structure nearby that reaches to its skirt tails. At 328 metres tall, it's the highest tower in all of the Southern Hemisphere, the twelfth highest in the world and, of course, "taller than Sydney's AMP Tower", a point that Sky City is eager to impress on its website. (There's that inferiority complex again…) Click through a couple more pages and you will find some very impressive facts and figures about the Sky Tower.

It was constructed from fifteen thousand cubic metres of high-strength, high-performance concrete, nearly two thousand tons of reinforcing steel and 650 tons of structural steel. It weighs 21,000 tons ("equivalent to 6,000 elephants"!) and its foundations sink down more than fifteen metres. The most sophisticated telemetry ever employed in New Zealand was used during its construction to ensure that it was plumb upright. On a clear day, an observer can see more than fifty miles from the tower, as far as Leigh Peninsula in the north and the Bombay Hills in the south. It has been designed and constructed to be able to withstand wind gusts of 200km/h as well as a magnitude 8.0 earthquake occurring within twenty kilometres. Its mast broadcasts seventeen stations, a world record for a single antenna. And so on...

This is one impressive building. But beyond the facts, the Sky Tower, which is essentially a casino and entertainment venue, has a particularly arresting visual impact from all round the city. You can see it from miles away and it is the only useful navigational aid in what is a surprisingly large city. At night it is lit in an array of bright and beautiful colours: greens, yellows, blues, red. And it spends every October bathed in eye-catching pink glow to mark Breast Cancer Awareness Month.

So where am I going with all this? Well, it's to make the point that the Auckland Sky Tower is about as out of place in Auckland as a building could be. It belongs in Shanghai or Kuala Lumpur or Miami maybe. But Auckland? No. It's like a lion among sheep. When I arrived in the city in 2000, five years since my last trip to the city, and three years since the Sky Tower opened to the public, the sight of the building astonished me. How could the relevant officials have approved its construction? Surely there was a public outcry – Kiwis love public outcries – over the sheer audacity of it? Because, to me, the tower stands as an ironic marker of the defining condition that affects New Zealand society: tall poppy syndrome.

A classic antipodean trait, which in its most positive guise might be defined as "backing the underdog", tall poppy syndrome (TPS) has come to assume perjorative connotations as the public scorning of the success of others. Under its effect, an individual who tries to rise above his economic, social or political standing is grappled back to Earth with a thud. Which is to say, it is egalitarianism at its worst.

Once a very Australian term, the Aussies seem to have got over their TPS in the last twenty years or so. Though theirs remains a mostly classless society, success is honoured and encouraged – the country's economic and cultural rise to prominence in the last decade pays testimony to that (and is no coincidence). So, despite efforts in some circles to identify and eradicate it in New Zealand, Kiwis have been left to carry the burden of tall poppy syndrome on their own. The result? Well, for one, only the All Blacks, winning America's Cup crew members and the most down-to-earth celebrities in the land – like Edmund Hillary, a Kiwi legend – are widely honoured in public, without qualification or criticism. But more pertinently than that, on a societal level, it goes much deeper, ultimately manifesting itself as an excuse for New Zealand mediocrity, both individually and as a people.

Why work longer hours than necessary when your colleagues are just going to disparage you for working too hard, for seeking the limelight? Why make an effort when effort isn't rewarded appropriately? Why even try something new if it points you out as different?

In a country where there is little dishonour in living on the dole, most Kiwis are happy to conform in all aspects of life, from clothing and appearances to work and even play. Combine this mindset with the climate, and ultimately you've got a country of people who are used to being bored. The kids survive by smoking dope and the adults get by on conversations about rugby, the weather and the latest spate of garden-hose theft. And, as such, tall poppy syndrome goes to the heart of much of what is foreign, and objectionable even, about New Zealand society from a South African point of view.

Of course, there are Kiwis who will object to this generalisation.

The extreme sports operators, for one. But they are simply the exception that proves the rule. The reason why New Zealand was the first country to run a commercial bungy jump, in the mid-eighties, is because there were enough of them who realised they had to do *something* to up their excitement levels. Yet another irony to add to the list. Otherwise, any Kiwi with ambition (and who isn't playing representative rugby) leaves the country after university to travel the world for ten years before coming home to settle down; or he emigrates for good to Australia, where close on four hundred thousand New Zealanders now live.

I met my fair share of Aucklanders who seemed conscious of the fact that Sydney had become a superior city to theirs on many levels. Their traditional Kiwi values seemed to compel them to reject Australia on principal and yet they all seemed to gaze longingly across the Tasman Sea. The resulting collective inferiority complex of New Zealand's primary city, caught between mediocrity and potential, is the final discouragement I required to ever want to settle there again.

If I do ever have to spend another extended spell in New Zealand, I shall make a point of heading down south. The South Islanders are, at least, an honest, decent, straightforward bunch, without pretence and content with themselves. But that, of course, is a hypothetical that I don't plan on fulfilling any time soon.

For the final take on Kiwi culture, let's return for a moment to the Sky Tower and those extreme-sports fanatics just mentioned, who've set up a "base-jump by wire" rig near the top. If you're in the mood, you can take a 192-metre jump off the tower, falling for about sixteen seconds – kind of like bungy jumping but upright. As marvellous as it sounds, you will be most happy to know that the whole set-up is OSH-approved. (That's Occupational Safety and Health, if you didn't know.) Also, besides the tremendous weather- and earthquake-survivability of the tower, there are extensive safety features to combat the unlikely event of fire. All features and figures mentioned far exceed the New Zealand Code Of Practice. Relief all round.

I mention these now because, should you ever make the move to New Zealand, you will suddenly find yourself a lot more concerned about such matters. In South Africa, we don't bother with petty safety considerations; we focus on not being hijacked in our driveways, not being ransacked at knifepoint, not being driven into by minibus taxis on the open road. Kiwis, though, have the luxury of fretting about where they swim, how to drive and when to check the weather report… Off the top of my head, here are some lines – accurate in my mind, at least – from New Zealand safety-awareness advertisements that I've watched over the years:

"Don't swim in the rip. If you do, you're a bloody idiot."

"Always wear your life jacket. Pinetree Meads does."

"Don't forget to brake before the bend."

"Always check the water before you dive in."

"Don't go out unless you've checked the forecast."

Give or take a word or two, these are real television advertisements that were played extensively – enough that I remember them. But as valid as all that advice is – yes, you *should* brake before going around a bend – is it really necessary? Do you have to be told that you shouldn't dive headfirst into shallow water? Do you really need Colin Meads to tell you that wearing a life jacket is a good idea when you're on the open sea in a dinghy? Life suddenly seems a lot less exciting when this is the advice you're getting on television. Surely, you can cut down on those expensive time-consuming advertisements and just let Darwin deal with the couple of morons who don't know that swimming in the rip isn't such a good idea?

And where does it end?

"Don't chop onions with your eyes shut."

"Don't put your hand in an open flame."

"Don't play in traffic."

"Don't bathe in warm water then slit your wrists parallel to your veins because you can't handle the boredom of living."

These seemingly arbitrary safety snippets once again illustrate the chasm between life there and life here. In *My Traitor's Heart*, Malan recalls Breyten Breytenbach's evocative description of the almost intangible feeling of South Africa: "heartspace and the danger of beauty". Malan himself touches on it with his notion of "the reckless jol". And while there is certainly beauty in New Zealand, it is limited in scope: lush, verdant, one-dimensional. South Africa is varied and vibrant, full of extremes: heat, drought, coldness, wetness. Diverse landscapes and possibilities across the country. Inspiration all around.

Just as it is human for us to identify potential dangers and judge them relative to others – swimming in the rip *is* comparatively dangerous in New Zealand – so it is human nature to worry. It's what we do to pass the time. So, around the average New Zealand dinner table, there may be serious talk of that horrific spate of garden-hose theft, and it will be in virtually the same tones as the standard South African horrific-spate-of-hijackings conversation. Johannesburg-Cape Town-Durban talk often revolves around the ever-present potential of violence in our daily lives or the seemingly endless procession of governmental corruption and incompetence that goes on unchecked, compared to the Auckland-Wellington-Christchurch discussions of neighbourhood grievances or Maori-welfare disputes – and yet the gravity of the conversations, half a world apart, are the same. The worry is universal.

Ominously, though, especially considering that the description of his longing for South Africa has stirred me in the past, Rian Malan stated in an article in *The Spectator* in late 2006 that he was planning on selling his Cape Town house and moving on from here.

It seems he no longer has the heart for "the reckless jol". Whether or not it was artistic licence – reinforcing what the blurb of his piece termed South Africa's "inexorable decline into disorder, political corruption and maladministration" – the suggestion seems to be that everyone reaches a point of collapse. And the older you are, the more likely it is to hit you.

When local horror talk does cross over into genuine daily fear, it seems, like modern terrorism, to be self-fulfilling. Just as terrorists have succeeded when airline passengers are body searched and made to carry their onboard luggage in see-through plastic bags, so South Africans have already lost to the carjackers and rapists and crooked politicians when they obsess about the stories of violence; when they fear to sleep in their own beds at night and fear that the country might fall apart at any second. And if this is you, then perhaps New Zealand is the better option. Perhaps when you have lived enough and experienced enough of Africa and South Africa, the "heartspace and the danger of beauty" runs out.

And so, just as I've conceded that New Zealand can make a very worthy holiday destination, I can't deny that if you are older and less prone to excitement these days, then perhaps the country does warrant consideration. There is most definitely crime there, but it is nothing on ours, and you will mostly feel safe walking in the streets (avoid south Auckland). But you will feel safe and bored. So if you do go, don't make the mistake that you are moving for the sake of your children; your child won't thank you if he ever realises what he's missing back home.

The last time I returned to Cape Town after a lengthy spell abroad, a year in Sydney, was in early 2006. Stepping off the plane into a hot Cape summer afternoon and looking up to Table Mountain in the distance, I got goosebumps like nothing else. It was one of those rare moments of emotion that, even as a man, you're proud to admit. Hell, the sight of the mountain very nearly brought tears to my eyes. And here's the thing: though I had been away for quite some time and this was a particularly meaningful return for me, *every time* I come back to Cape Town, whether by plane or car, after a weekend or a year, the sight of that reassuring, steadfast rock prickles my skin and welcomes me back. I expect it. It's what coming home feels like.

But whenever I get off the plane in Auckland and take the long ride into the city, I half expect to look to where the Sky Tower once stood and see that it's been chopped down while I was gone.

New Zealand is a country of thirty thousand million sheep,
three million of whom think they are human.

– Barry Humphries

New Zealand was colonized initially by those Australians who
had the initiative to escape.

– Robert Muldoon

If an English butler and an English nanny sat down to design
a country, they would come up with New Zealand.

– Anonymous

ALSO BY TWO DOGS...

Modern Man is a Wimp...
– Long Live Real Men!
By John Shannan

Who'd want to be a man today?
Women scorn them, advertisers belittle
them and pop culture claims they're the
root of all evil. They're judged by the
labels they wear and the moisturisers
they use, and all about them lurks
political correctness... How has it come
to this? Why is life so different from 30
years ago? John Shannan looks for the
answers – and some male respite in this
increasingly insane world.

ISBN 978-1-92013-710-6

Hijack!
By Guy Brown

Car hijacking is the culturally defining
crime of contemporary South Africa.
Now, for the first time, a renowned SA
investigative journalist has interviewed
carjackers and the cops who hunt
them to piece together a semi-fictional
account of the dismantling of a Gauteng
syndicate. Blending fact and fiction, as
well as our turbulent past and turbulent
present, this is riveting, insightful
reading for men.

ISBN 1-92013-713-0

ALSO BY TWO DOGS...

Don't Climb Kili…
Climb The Ruwenzori
By Fiona McIntosh and Tim Richman
A dose of inspiration for South
Africans looking for holidays that are
exactly that: holidays – not familiar
treks along well-beaten paths teeming
with hordes of tourists and their
annoying kids… Anyone who has ever
climbed Kilimanjaro will know the
feeling: yes, it's an accomplishment
getting to the top, but so is coping
with 300 hikers at every camp site.
Whether it's a mountain, a town, a
wine estate, a beach or a hiking trail,
there are the tourist traps and there are
the little-known gems. Take your pick.

ISBN 1-92013-709-2

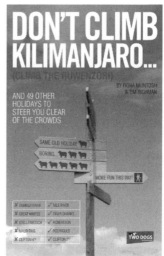

My Dad
By South African Sons
A compilation of the writings of
a broad range of celebrities and
authors from differing cultural
and religious backgrounds within
South Africa, *My Dad* is a moving,
thoughtful and insightful look at the
relationship between South African
men and their fathers. These are
sometimes tragic, sometimes
hilarious investigations into the
relationship that plays such an
important role in defining every
man. Contributors include Lucas
Radebe, Kevin Fine, Neil McCarthy,
Sean O'Toole and Justin Fox.

ISBN 1-920137-03-3

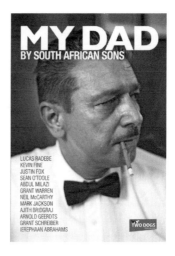

ALSO BY TWO DOGS...

293 Things Every SA Man Should Know
By Dennis Cavernelis

Exactly what it says, this book is a compilation of 293 utterly indispensable snippets of knowledge for the South African man – from worldly wisdom and sage advice to good-humoured observation and trivial facts. But it's not as straightforward as all that... There's zombie-killing advice, jump-starting advice and cigar-lighting advice. There are facts to remember, facts to forget and facts to drop at fancy dinner parties. An ideal gift and even a conversation piece, this is the thinking man's light read.

ISBN 1-920137-01-7

Getting Away With Murder...
By Rick Crosier

Getting Away with Murder: The Slacker's Guide To Getting Away With As Much As Possible is everyman's guide to glossing over those little life technicalities that tend to hold us back from time to time. The GAWM way of life means never having to say sorry again – because no-one really expects too much from you in the first place... Sharp, witty and entertaining, this is the advice you need to make your life that much more manageable. Hey, everyone else is doing, so why don't you?

ISBN 1-92013-707-6

ALSO BY TWO DOGS...

Women's Bodies
– A User's Manual
By Kerry Rogers

Charting a course from head to toe (including all the important bits in between), *Women's Bodies: A User's Manual* is the definitive guide for men to the female body. The ins and outs of all the vital erogenous zones are touched upon – with just the right amount of pressure – offering the information a well-read gentleman needs for better sex. Smart, sexy and informative, this is a book men will use and women will thank them for.

ISBN 1-920137-06-8

In Search of South Africa's Perfect Woman
By Kevin McCallum

Every single man is in search of the perfect woman – and they need all the help they can get. As the ultimate sports-loving single guy, Kevin McCallum is the archetypal SA bachelor. Here, as he charts his tortuous path through our dating highways and byways, from dingy bars to more respectable social occasions, there are lessons to be learnt, pains to be shared and laughs to be snorted down with an ice-cold beer. Does the perfect woman even exist? Of course she does! Er, doesn't she?

ISBN 1-920137-04-1

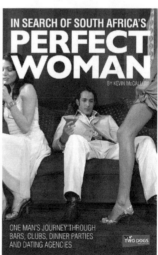

ALSO BY TWO DOGS...

Sports Holidays
– Where To Go And When
By Kevin McCallum and Rowan Cory
A compilation of the most exciting
local and international sporting
events for South African men to
watch or participate in over the next
two years, *Sports Holidays* will inform,
inspire and motivate you to go on
that dream trip you always wanted
– or to simply to get away for a
weekend. Chapters are introduced
by renowned sports writer Kevin
McCallum, whereafter all the
necessary info for a great tour,
whether it's playing or watching,
is included.

ISBN 1-920137-05X

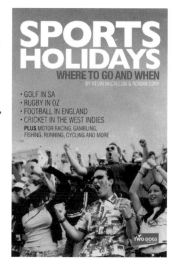

I Can Do That
– Fitness For The Lazy Guy
By Blair Ludbrook
This is the book that every stressed
out, unhealthy South African guy
needs to prod him off the couch and
into a healthier lifestyle. Taking a
complete approach, from psychology
and nutrition to training and
event listings, it gives readers the
knowledge and motivation to take
the jump from lazy couch potato
to half-marathon runner or regular
surf-skier – while still enjoying a beer
or two. There's no preaching here:
just an achievable, practical recipe
for success.

ISBN 1-920137-02-5

FOR MORE INFORMATION ON TWO DOGS VISIT
www.twodogs.co.za